D1189971

THE LAKELAND FELLS ALMANAC

Bill Birkett

Neil Wilson Publishing • Glasgow • Scotland

© Bill Birkett, 1997

Published by Neil Wilson Publishing Ltd
303a The Pentagon Centre
36 Washington Street
GLASGOW
G3 8AZ
Tel: 0141-221-1117
Fax: 0141-221-5363
E-mail: nwp@cqm.co.uk
http://www.nwp.co.uk/

The author asserts his moral right to be identified
as the author of this work

A CIP catalogue record for this book is available
from the British Library.

ISBN 1-897784-59-7

All photos by Bill Birkett Photo Library

Typeset in 8 on 8.3pt Bodoni.
Printed in the UAE by Oriental Press

AUTHOR'S DISCLAIMER

Although the author encountered no difficulty of access on the routes
described, and while considerable effort has been made to avoid so doing,
the inclusion of a walk in the book does not imply that a right of way exists
in every case. Any known problems at the time of writing have been
highlighted and it is up to the individual to make their own decision.

Readers are also advised that changes can occur to the landscape
which may effect the contents of this book. The author
welcomes notification of any such changes.

CONTENTS

SOUTHERN FELLS

INTRODUCTION

Despite the massive amount of material available on the magnificent Lakeland hills I have felt frustrated for a long time with its random distribution, eccentricity, and frequently monochrome outlook. What I thought would be appreciated was a book logically structured to give the whole picture – not just another selective and incomplete work but one both comprehensive and accurately detailed. This approach resulted in *Complete Lakeland Fells* first published in 1994, identifying all the 541 independent fell tops.

I intended it to be the definitive book based on a lifetime's experience on the fells. Written and photographed with a will to serve them justly; a work containing the most complete information available. Judging by the very positive reviews, letters, comments and popularity of *Complete Lakeland Fells*, it appears that I succeeded. Of course a reference work of that magnitude is too bulky to be carried around and cannot be considered to be a practical fieldbook and so I set my mind to trying to condense and distil the essential elements of the book into a handier format. Neil Wilson already publishes Cameron McNeish's ideal rucksack 'almanacs' to Scotland's Munros and Corbetts and we decided that there was no reason why we could not extend the same treatment to the Lakeland Fells.

The Lakeland Fells Almanac has been written and formatted to comply precisely with the 'almanac' approach. Designed for use on the fell, it describes routes to all 541 fell tops over 1000 feet in the Lake District National Park. In all, 129 circular walks are described, covering all the tops. These walks have been selected both for their quality and practicality.

Many have set their sights on ascending all the 541 tops I originally listed and numerous people are referring to them as the Birketts. So be it. To date information is scant, I have no information as to anyone ascending all these tops, and it would be a useful exercise to record those who (if any bar myself) have completed them. So if you have a mind to, please send names, dates and times to Bill Birkett via NWP marked 'Lakeland Fells Records'. For my part, and by way of encouragement, I offer to buy a traditional pint of bitter or cider for the first ten persons who have successfully visited all the separate tops. An act of unparalleled generosity.

NOTES ON USING THIS BOOK

Whilst *Complete Lakeland Fells* defines the order of the fell tops in terms of six areas (Western, North-Western, Northern, Central, Eastern and Southern Fells) and 36 groups and offers lists of the tops in order of altitude (by group and overall), the principle of this book is that it should be portable and of real use on the hills. Each group of fells has a map, a photograph (where space permits), and suggested bases and suitable accommodation. Walks are then described which collectively cover routes to all the tops within the group. For each walk/route the tops are listed in order of arrival, with their height and grid reference, the OS map(s) required, the access point, the distance and ascent involved with an approximate time given for completing the route. Any known access problems are summarised. Miles and kilometres are quoted as well as feet and metres.

The route descriptions are summaries of the best way I think to tackle all 541 tops. Some may want to tackle more tops per outing, others less, but I strove to balance longer expeditions with shorter evening or half-day trips. These descriptions should only be used as a guide, in conjunction with the appropriate Ordnance Survey (OS) map.

Please note that the abbreviation NWWA stands for North-West Water Authority.

ACCESS

Along with the founding principles of the National Parks for England and Wales it has long been established that the right of free access exists to and on the Lakeland Fells. Whilst many of us regard the fells as 'God-given' and maintain we have a moral 'right' to roam, it should be appreciated that to a certain extent this happy state of access is due to the goodwill of private landowners, local farmers, and careful management by The National Parks Authority and The National Trust. We, as hill-walkers, should respect this and, as individuals, do our utmost to maintain the environment and respect people's privacy. The ideal we should adopt is to take only photographs and leave as little trace of our passing as possible. Every user of this book should be familiar with and adhere rigidly to the Country Code.

Sadly a few landowners/tenants are worried about the increasing numbers of walkers on the fells and are anxious to bar access. Any such known access problems have been indicated in the individual route summary. However it should also be appreciated that in addition to any green line indicating known public rights of way on the OS maps and above the general principal of open access on the fells, there are other criteria that define a Public Right of Way and free access. One such is that if a route has been used in 'custom and practice' for 20 years then a de facto right of way exists. In each route where access problems have been detailed in this book the author believes the latter to be the case; an immediate indication being the fact that the routes have been previously described in guidebooks over 20 years ago.

Erosion can be a problem and for the wider good of the fells one should comply with any upland management schemes that are in progress. The National Parks Authority and The National Trust have done much excellent work in restoring footpaths and preventing further erosion. They do this for our benefit as hill lovers and they deserve every assistance we can give them.

1 DERWENT WATER/THIRLMERE FELLS

Location: Lying on the eastern edge of the Western Fells, this upland tongue protrudes northwards between Borrowdale/Derwent Water to the west and Thirlmere to the east.

Suggested Bases: Keswick, Borrowdale and Thirlmere.

Accommodation: Keswick: all facilities except railway station; Longthwaite youth hostel; camping at The Headlands (Derwent Water), Castlerigg Hall and Castlerigg Farm. *Borrowdale:* Barrow House youth hostel; b&b at The Scafell Inn; camping at Ashness Farm, Dalt Wood-Grange, Stonethwaite, Thornythwaite and Seathwaite farms. Bus service from Keswick. *Thirlmere:* Youth hostel; b&b at the King's Head Inn; camping at Bridge End Farm and Dale Bottom. Bus service from Ambleside to Keswick.

WALLA CRAG, 1234FT/376M; BLEABERRY FELL, 1935FT/590M; HIGH SEAT, 1995FT/608M

Maps: OS OL4, L90: GR 277213, GR 286196, GR 287181
Access point: Great Wood car park, GR 272212
Distance/ascent: 6¼ mls/2000ft; 10km/610m
Approx time: 4 hours

Leave the car park by the stile and follow the track forking right to Cat Gill. Follow the path steeply up the north bank of the gill to emerge through pines; bear left up the open shoulder. A stile, through a gap in the stone wall on the left, leads to a path following the wall with occasional views through the trees which soon disappear. Rejoin main path and you reach the open bare rock top of Walla Crag.

Backtrack for a short way to the first break in the stone wall and follow the well-defined path traversing the upper reaches of Cat Gill to Bleaberry Fell. With a number of minor variations possible, the path stretches along the broad ridge to High Seat. A post and wire fence marks most of the route, though whichever route is followed, bog will be encountered before the rocky bumps of Threefooted Brandreth are crossed to gain the summit and triangulation point.

Descend to a little hollow and more bog before a well-defined path crosses a ruined stone wall to descend into the upper regions of Ashness Gill. To visit the cairned small rocky oucrops marking the possible top of Ashness Fell, make a detour left. The bump in the shoulder below these is known simply as Dodd. A steep descent leads back to the path. After the initial section of gill, at the head of a sizeable waterfall, bear left. Descend down the flanks of the gill past rock, bracken and tree. Descend a short section of road until a track bears right (signposted 'Great Wood and Keswick') to climb a stile. The low track contours the hillside beneath Falcon

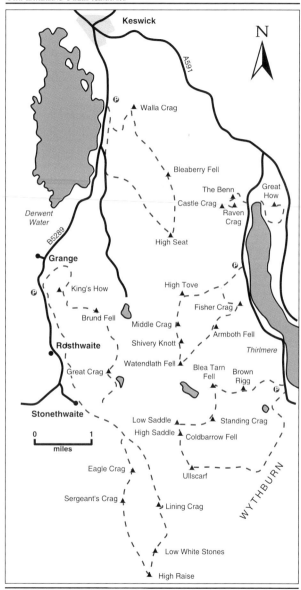

Crags to regain Great Wood. A footbridge crosses over Cat Gill to the original track.

RAVEN CRAG, 1512FT/461M; CASTLE CRAG (SHOULTHWAITE), 1381FT/421M; THE BENN, 1463FT/446M

Maps: OS OL4, L90: GR 303187, GR 300183, GR 302193
Access point: Car park at the western end of Thirlmere Dam
    GR 307189
Distance/ascent: 2mls/425ft; 3.5km/128m
Approx time: 2 hours

Leave the parking space walking north along the road for about 100 metres where a sign 'Castle Crag Ancient Monument' directs you left through a little gate. Steep going up a rough path leads through pines to a forest track. This loops up the hillside taking you directly beneath the sheer north-east face of Raven Crag, then back again into the pines. Soon, as you begin to encounter larch, a diagonal path joins the track from the left. Follow this. It rises rapidly, with beech taking over from conifer, to reach a shoulder and another wide forest track. Bear left on this and almost immediately leave it on the left to find a path leading up a tiny valley to the top of Raven Crag. Take great care for the unguarded vertical rock face lies directly below.

Retrace your steps to the track. A sign points to the rocky bump of Castle Crag Fort. Ascending in a clockwise direction reveals a level platform guarded by grassed-over remnants of a boundary wall and strange earthworks. A short scramble gains the summit of the final rocky knoll. Walk north to find an easy traverse leading back to the original point of ascent.

Return to the main forest track and follow this north for a few hundred metres until a slight path bears off to the right which follows roughly the crest of the shoulder, through the pines, until the steep slopes that mark the top of The Benn are reached. The path runs up to the right, bypassing the steep scree, to the hollowed-out summit cone. Descend to the north following a narrow path and occasional marker post. Soon this intercepts a forestry track – the original track followed during the ascent.

GREAT HOW, 1100FT/335M

Maps: OS OL4, L90: GR 314188
Access point: Car park at the western end of Thirlmere Dam,
    GR 307189
Distance/ascent: 3mls/430ft; 5km/130m
Approx time: 1¹/₂ hours

Cross the dam to find steps and the 'Permissive Path Dalehead Swirls' sign on the right. Traverse the bank of the reservoir until the path breaks away from the water's edge. Contour the hillside to find a track bearing up to the left. As the track becomes overgrown a sign marks a path 'Great How Summit' which leads up to the right. In a short while the rocky top is reached. Descend to the base of the How; return in the same direction. Alternatively strike anticlockwise along the track until the road is reached.

HIGH TOVE, 1689FT/515M; MIDDLE CRAG 1587FT/484M; SHIVERY KNOTT, 1610FT/491M; WATENDLATH FELL, 1689FT/515M; ARMBOTH FELL, 1570FT/479M; FISHER CRAG, 1381FT/421M

Maps: OS OL4, L90: GR 289165, GR 288158, GR 289154, GR 289148, GR 297159, GR 305163
Access point: Armboth Car Park, GR 306172
Distance/ascent: 5mls/1340ft; 8km/425m
Approx time: 3$\frac{1}{2}$ hours

Cross the road from the car park; a wooden sign reads 'Public Footpath Watendlath'. Go over a bridge, passing some boulders before the path rises steeply. At the top of the rise, right of the gill and plantation, the path leads through a gap in the stone wall. Beyond this a vague path leads to the summit cairn of High Tove.

Watendlath lies directly below but bear left along the flat and boggy watershed. The post and wire fence line offers some possibility to wire-walk the wettest sections before the rocky knoll of Middle Fell rises to its right. Scale the fence to reach it; move on to the next rocky outcrop of Shivery Knott and beyond that the substantial rocky plateau of Watendlath Fell. Clamber over the fence to a cairn on its west spur for views of quiet Blea Tarn.

Head north east for Armboth Fell over thick heather. Descend into a small basin and cross the stream. Rising from the stream, an ancient cairn covered in green lichen stands to the right. The summit of Armboth Fell will be found on the most northerly outcrop of rock, on the left edge of the upland mass now in front. A tiny cairn marks it.

Strike east. Heather, rock, tarns and pines give the scene a strong Scottish flavour. Take care not to fall over the small but precipitous crags on the descent towards Fisher Crag. In the heathery hollow at the base of the shoulder walk around the right side of the tarn. To reach the top of Fisher Crag, scale the wire fence and probe the perimeter conifers to cross a broken stone wall. Ascend to find the rocky knoll swathed in vegetation. Return the same way before a course due west is taken which rises to a rocky knoll. An easy gully breaks down to the left after which a circular traverse is made. To cross the main source of Fisher Gill, keep reasonably high. Continue traversing to cross the second source of the gill and regain the original path at the head of the plantation.

BROWN RIGG, 1519FT/463M; BLEA TARN FELL, 1830FT/558M; STANDING CRAG, 2005FT/611M; LOW SADDLE of COLDBARROW FELL, 2152FT/656M; HIGH SADDLE of COLDBARROW FELL, 2215FT/675M; ULLSCARF, 2382FT/726M; WYTHBURN FELL, 1667FT/508M

Maps: OS OL4, L90: GR 305146, GR 298143, GR 296134,
    GR 288133, GR 289129, GR 292122, GR 312125
Access point: Dobgill Car Park, GR 316140
Distance/ascent: 6mls/2230ft; 10km/680m
Approx time: 4 hours

Should Dobgill be full, a short walk north along the road reveals another parking place and beyond this an area of fell, devoid of conifers. Take the stile leading over the fence and enter a walled but now redundant lane. Leave it by a wall-gap and continue up the hillside to find a tight ring of iron railing protecting what was once perhaps a well. Gain the track and bear right crossing a small embankment bridge to find a small gate above to the left. Climb steeply and find the remnants of an old zigzagging path. As the angle slackens beyond the top of Bank Crags, over to the right, pass a ruined building. Make a leftward trending traverse, above the forestry, aiming for the distinctive balanced rock marking the summit of Brown Rigg.

Descend to Stone Hause then begin the ascent of Blea Tarn Fell by the broad rake on the left. Soon it becomes easier to avoid the short rocky buttresses by circumnavigating them to the right. The summit of Blea Tarn Fell (unnamed on OS map) reveals a trig point and on its most northerly point, a naturally curved rock seat. The ascent to the rocky bastion of Standing Crag is steep but is a worthy prize after which a traverse across to the distinct Low Saddle top of Coldbarrow Fell is easily made.

The boulder cluster of High Saddle follows. A flattish walk, eventually guided (useful in the mist) by old iron posts, leads to the summit cairn of Ullscarf. The route, no definite path, lies east in the direction of Seat Sandal and Fairfield. Skirt Black Knott to gain the long curving ridge situated above Wythburn valley. Descend the ridge keeping near its edge to pass a shepherd's cairn placed on an indefinite top. Below lies the rocky lump of Wythburn Fell top and beyond lies the beacon marked on the map. Beneath this a long-forgotten grassed track leads through a gap in the wall. Follow the deer fence crossing a subsidiary fence to gain and follow the line of the old wall. A gate gives access through the deer fence to Harrop Tarn. Take the track and cross the exit stream. Turn right immediately and follow the constructed path by Dob Gill down through the conifers.

KING'S HOW on GRANGE FELL, 1286FT/392M; BRUND FELL, 1363FT/415M;
GREAT CRAG (STONETHWAITE), 1444FT/440M

Maps: OS OL4, L90: GR 258166, GR 265163, GR 270147
Access point: The Bowderstone Car Park, GR 253168
Distance/ascent: 6¹/2 mls/1625ft; 10.5km/495m
Approx time: 4 hours

From the top corner of the car park take the stile over the
fence. A well-defined path crosses a small stream and proceeds
gently at first past some old quarry workings. A steady pull
leads to an open shoulder. Dropping from the shoulder through the
stone wall the path enters the thickly wooded head of Troutdale.
Bearing right, it soon begins to climb steeply through the trees to
emerge onto an open shoulder. Continue to a wire fence and bear
right along it. Climb to gain a small boggy valley between rocky
hummocks. Bear right to cross only the end of the valley. A stout
yew tree on the left marks the way before the path contours the
hillside. Continue to the Borrowdale face of the fell and rise to the
summit cairn of King's How.

Descend and traverse the path along the fell to the end of the
shoulder of Brund Fell. Bear left ascending to pass through the
rock outcrops. Finally climb to the cairned highest point
immediately above the path.

Descend to a wall and follow it down on the Watendlath side,
boggy in places, to cross the main Rosthwaite/Watendlath track in
the hollow. Opposite lies a kissing gate and beyond a path
continues, aiming ultimately for an obvious small valley weakness
in the next section of raised fell. Before this is reached a detour
sign will be found directing you leftwards to circumnavigate the
bog in front. A kissing gate through the stone wall gives access to
the weakness in the hillside and the ascent is made. At the top of
the slope where the cairned main path levels, leave it and strike up
rightwards through thick heather and rough ground to find the
summit of Great Crag (there is no real path). Below lies Dock
Tarn. After a boggy section midway along the tarn, the
unmistakeable path leads over the edge of the fell. An uneven rock
staircase descends through the wood to join the main track along
the valley floor. Level walking leads pleasantly to Rosthwaite.

Our way continues to the right. Initially follow the track to
Watendlath. The track emerges from the trees and begins to rise
up the hillside. Leave it and bear left along by the post and wire
fence. Eventually the road is joined at a small car park. Walk
along the pavement on the left of the road until a stile/wooden gate
gives access to a rocky track on the right. This leads to the huge
Bowderstone. The track continues past a small rock face to the
right and then a large slate quarry, before regaining the car park.

EAGLE CRAG, 1709FT/521M; SERGEANT'S CRAG, 1873FT/571M; HIGH
RAISE, 2500FT/762M; LOW WHITE STONES, 2398FT/731M; LINING CRAG,
1778FT/542M

Maps: OS OL4, L90: GR 276121, GR 274114, GR 281095,
    GR 282101, GR 283112
Access point: Limited car parking in the centre of the hamlet of
    Stonethwaite by the telephone kiosk, GR 262137
Distance/ascent: 7mls/2,500ft; 11.5km/762m
Approx time: 4¹/2 hours

Follow the track over Stonethwaite Bridge and turn right,
continuing along the lane. Cross the bridge over Greenup Gill
and find a small stile over the post and wire fence on the left.
Continue along a path passing through two stone walls. At the
second wall turn right, making a strenuous ascent directly up the
hillside. At the top of the wall bear left until the higher wall of the
enclosure can be crossed where it meets the crag on the left. Bear
right onto the shoulder to find a short gully through the craggy
ground above. Climb this to the shoulder until it is possible to
traverse right under a rock face. The path continues through
easier terraces to reach the angled rock slab and cairn that marks
the summit of Eagle Crag.

Descent of this section is not advised without prior knowledge.
Aiming for Sergeant's Crag move down to the corner of the wall.
Continue along this, eventually deviating rightwards to gain the
summit of Sergeant's Crag. The way is now straightforward,
leading across the final section of the spur to join the flanks of
High Raise. Keep Long Crag to your left but gain the shoulder
above, then bear easily right to the summit of High Raise -- the
highest point of the fell and of the boulder field named High White
Stones.

A broad path leads back along to the cairned hump of Low
White Stones and down Greenup Edge. In the hollow bear left and
follow the cairned path to the narrow-edged top of Lining Crag.
Beware here, a cliff lies directly below. Turn right to find a paved
staircase spiralling safely down the north side of the crag. The
path continues through an interesting area of humped moraine
through the narrow valley of Greenup Gill. Soon the original track
is joined.

2 LANGDALE FELLS

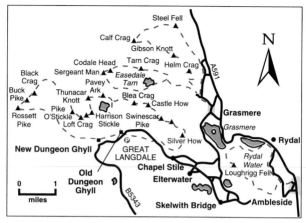

Location: A triangular cluster of fells found between the
    Great Langdale and Grasmere Valleys.
Suggested Bases: Great Langdale, Ambleside and Grasmere.
Accommodation: Great Langdale: self-catering accommodation
    and b&b at The Old Dungeon Ghyll and Stickle Barn Inns
    (the latter with bunkhouse), Elterwater and Langdale (High
    Close) youth hostels. Camping at head of Great Langdale,
    Baysbrown Farm, Neaum Crag above Skelwith Bridge. Bus
    service from Ambleside to the Old Dungeon Ghyll. *Ambleside:*
    all facilities except railway station and campsite. Ambleside
    (Waterhead) youth hostel. *Grasmere:* plentiful accommodation
    though limited facilities. No railway station and no campsite.
    Butterlip Howe and Thorney How youth hostels.

HELM CRAG, 1329FT/405M; GIBSON KNOTT, 1384FT/422M; CALF CRAG,
1762FT/537M; DEAD PIKE on STEEL FELL, 1812FT/553M

Maps: OS OL4, OL7, L90: GR326094, GR 317100, GR 3402104,
    GR 319111
Access point: Car park on the Easedale Road above Grasmere,
    GR 334080
Distance/ascent: 7mls/2035ft; 11.5km/620m
Approx time: 4½ hours

An iron gate takes the road through meadows to the last
hamlet of Easedale. Follow the track through a further gate
before taking the right-hand lane leading onto open fellside
and the site of the old quarries. The path has been re-routed and

no longer traverses right to ascend the nose of Helm Crag directly. Instead it winds left zigzagging above Jackdaw Crag before returning to the original path at an open shoulder above the rocky knoll of White Crag. A steepish ascent leads to the first rocky pinnacle at the south-east end of the summit ridge.

Traverse to reach the actual summit, the second pinnacle of which is known as the Howitzer. It is necessary to make a short climb to reach the top. A steep descent leads to the col of Bracken Hause above Far Easedale. The path mostly traverses below the bumpy crest, but don't miss the cairned top of Gibson Knott to the right. At the far end, passing the shapely Pike of Carrs to the left, the rocky summit of Calf Crag is reached. A gentle descent leads towards the tarn on Brownrigg Moss, swinging right after a short way to gain the remnants of an old iron fence -- the old county boundary between Westmorland to the south and Cumberland to the north. Following the fence line notice a fine little tarn to the left.

An easy ascent leads to the summit of Steel Fell (marked as Dead Pike on the OS map). Three paths lead from the summit. Bear right and take the one which descends Cotra Breast. This can be slippery when wet. The path returns to the road just below the large house of Helmside. Follow it back beneath Helm Crag to pass Underhelm Farm. Join the Easedale road just above Goody Bridge.

LOUGHRIGG, 1101FT/335M

Maps: OS OL7, L90: GR 347051
Access point: Central Car Park, Ambleside, GR 376047
Distance/ascent: 6mls/985ft; 9.5km/300m
Approx time: 3 hours

From the car park in Ambleside take the road towards Grasmere, passing the Fire and Police Stations. Bear left on the lane through the houses to find the path along the banks of Stock Ghyll to its confluence with the River Rothay. Slate-arched Miller Bridge crosses the river. Bear right, over the cattle grid. Almost immediately a surfaced lane leads steeply up to the left. Follow this, through a gate past a converted farm. At a bend in the road a stile and path will be found on the left. This leads between Miller How Wood above and Loughrigg Brow Wood below. A squeeze stile through a stone wall leads to open fell. Rising steeply, take the left branch in the path. Gain a rocky outcrop. Now follow the path rightwards to pass the bank of Lily Tarn and continue over the undulations passing a rocky tarn on the right before making a descent into a broad valley. Keep straight across this to take the path rising steeply up the hill on its far side. More undulations, passing tiny tarns, are traversed until the summit point is reached.

A steep descent leads to the end of Lougrigg Terrace. A high-level track traverses above Rydal Water to the great open slate

LANGDALE PIKES

quarry of Rydal Cave. Beyond this the track descends and
continues to another track leading through a gate and woods to the
surfaced road. Bear right at the bottom by Pelter Bridge and
follow the road back to Miller Bridge.

SILVER HOW, 1294FT/395M; LANG HOW, 1358FT/414M; SWINESCAR PIKE,
1348FT/411M; CASTLE HOW, 1640FT/500M; BLEA RIGG, 1776FT/541M

Maps: OS OL6, L90: GR 325066, GR 318071, GR 313072,
    GR 308076, GR 302078
Access point: Small parking space by road beneath Robinson
    Place Farm, GR 312062, alternatively the car park in front of
    The New Dungeon Ghyll Hotel, GR 296064
Distance/ascent: 6¼ mls/1475ft, 10km/450m
Approx time: 3½ hours

The point where the old road up the Great Langdale Valley
leaves the present is a good place to begin. Follow the new
road until just past Harry Place Farm. Opposite the barn a
path leads up left under two trees. At the wall find a gate leading
to open fellside and an excellent path. It traverses along a natural
line behind the rocky bump of Thrang Crag to gain Megs Gill.
Cross the steep scree-filled gill and rise steeply to gain the cairned
top of a grassy bump before traversing right to find the cairned
summit.

Bear left to regain the main path towards the elongated cone
of Lang How. Descend bearing left to a rocky knoll and then
beyond this, to the curious bump of Swinescar Pike.

After completing the circuit of the bog a path rises diagonally
rightwards across rocky scree to crest Little Castle How just below
its summit. A slight descent leads to the hollow area between the

three summits of Castle How. The highest, according to the OS is that on the left, Castle How. However, the most interesting is the small distinct rock summit over to the right -- Great Castle How. After a short way a path bears left and descends to Stickle Tarn. Descent down the true left bank of Stickle Ghyll involves a short section of easy scrambling by the side of Tarn Crag but is thereafter on constructed paths and is straightforward. Nearing the base of the ghyll cross the footbridge and continue descending to the New Dungeon Ghyll Hotel. Continue down the front drive to cross the main road into a car park to find the old road.

TARN CRAG, 1807FT/551M; CODALE HEAD, 2401FT/732M; SERGEANT MAN, 2414FT/736M

Maps: OS OL6, OL7, L90: GR 303094, GR 289091, GR 286089
Access point: Car park on the Easedale Road above Grasmere, GR 334080
Distance/ascent: 7mls/2165ft; 11km/660m
Approx time: 4 hours

At the bend in the road, opposite a postbox set in the stone wall, enter the wood on the far side of Easedale Beck. Cross the wooden footbridge. Exit the wood by an iron gate and follow the rocky track which in turn follows the bank of the beck. Fine views to the tumbling waterfalls of Sourmilk Gill soon come into view. The track bears left and rises beside the gill.

Above the falls, ringed by juniper and holly and where the path begins to steepen, bear right to cross the stream on stepping stones. In spate this will be impossible; in normal conditions it is a relatively simple affair. A small path rises up the fine open east ridge of Tarn Crag.

The steep bastion straight ahead looks difficult enough but a rake cuts easily up its centre. Move right and ascend to the rocky top of Tarn Crag.

The edge now broadens and the path becomes a little vague. No problems should be encountered to find the line of the old iron fence posts leading rightwards to the summit of Codale Head. Although following the old boundary will lead to the summit of High Raise, it is a traverse of rocky outcrops which leads to Sergeant Man.

On descent from the summit cairn a prominent path traverses a boggy area in front of Sergeant Man before heading down the ridge towards Blea Rigg. A long rock slab, of no difficulty, is followed by a hollow and a view to Codale Tarn. Numerous cairns mark this spot, an important cross-roads. Nevertheless it is easy to pass it by and continue down the ridge leading to Blea Rigg. Take great care not to do this, but bear left immediately to make a steep descent. The path levels out before a further steep section contains rocky steps. Continue to traverse above the shoreline of Easedale and descend by Sourmilk Gill.

PAVEY ARK, 2288FT/697M; THUNACAR KNOTT, 2372FT/723M; HARRISON STICKLE, 2414FT/736M; THORN CRAG, 2106FT/642M; LOFT CRAG, 2238FT/682M; PIKE O'STICKLE, 2324FT/709M; BLACK CRAG (MICKLEDEN), 1929FT/588M; BUCK PIKE (MICKLEDEN), 1988FT/606M; ROSSETT PIKE, 2136FT/651M

Maps: OS OL6, L90: GR 285079, GR 279080, GR 282074, GR 280072, GR 275071, GR 274075, GR 282074, GR 253078, GR 249076

Access point: Car Park beside the Stickle Barn/New Dungeon Ghyll Hotel, GR 295064

Distance/ascent: 9mls/3460ft, 14.5km/1055m

Approx time: 5½ hours

A reconstructed path leads up Stickle Ghyll to pass under Tarn Crag and arrive at Stickle Tarn on the east end of the dam. Traverse above the eastern shore until, bearing left, the path crosses its main feeder stream – Bright Beck. Soon a good path up the easy eastern shoulder of Pavey Ark is followed. A little wall on the left is crossed to gain the rock summit. Head west towards Thunacar Knott and pick up a path before moving left to the highest point south of the little tarn. North of the tarn there's also a cairned top, sometimes regarded as 'the' top although it is a lower point. A path storms directly across to make the slight ascent to Harrison Stickle. A cairn on the northern end of a rocky ridge marks the summit and the highest point of The Langdale Pikes.

Descend into the hollow above the deep-cut rocky ravine of Dungeon Ghyll. Rising from the stream the cairned head of Thorn Crag presents no problems before the path bears west up to Loft Crag. The path continues to skirt the top of the Stickle Stone Shoot before climbing steeply up the rocky summit cone of Pike O'Stickle. Descend Pike O'Stickle only by the same route taken in ascent. Our path continues across Martcrag Moor to round the hidden hollow of Stake Pass. Ascending up and left leads to the rocky top of Black Crag. In turn reach Buck Pike and airy Rossett Pike. Descend the grassy back of the Pike before aiming down the red scree of Rossett Gill. Care is required here. Levelling out, the path passes over a little footbridge before following along the bank of Mickleden Beck. Soon the grassy greensward of Mickleden valley is followed by a rocky lane to the Old Dungeon Ghyll Hotel. By skirting above the buildings to the left, signposted, the lane can be regained and followed back to Stickle Barn/New Dungeon Ghyll car park.

3 BOWFELL GROUP

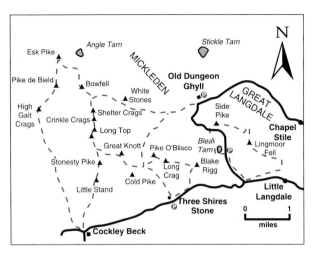

Location: Rising between the heads of Great Langdale and Eskdale
and terminating along the Little Langdale – Wrynose Pass,
southern boundary of the Western Fells.

Suggested Bases: Great Langdale, Little Langdale.

Accommodation: *Great Langdale:* self-catering accommodation
and b&b; The Old Dungeon Ghyll and Stickle Barn Inns (the
latter with bunkhouse); Elterwater and Langdale (High Close)
youth hostels; camping at head of Great Langdale, Baysbrown
Farm, Neaum Crag above Skelwith Bridge. Bus service from
Ambleside to the Old Dungeon Ghyll. *Little Langdale:* limited
self-catering and b&b at The Three Shires Inn.

BROWN HOWE on LINGMOOR FELL, 1538FT/469M; SIDE PIKE,
1187FT/362M

Maps: OS OL6, L90: GR 303046, GR 293054
Access point: Blea Tarn Car Park, GR 296043
Distance/ascent: 5¼ mls/1410ft, 8.5km/430m
Approx time: 3 hours

Take the road to cross the cattle-grid and descend the hill.
A little way above a lower cattle-grid a grassy track leads off to
the left (a low barrier prevents vehicular access). This climbs
to a flat area (there is a gate in the wall on the left), then descends
slightly to a gate in the fence. Contour around to cross the beck
just above the wall and trees. A rocky step leads to a well-defined

path contouring the flanks of Lingmoor above the fell wall. Pass beneath Busk Pike and Bield Crag (the buildings of High and Low Bield lie just below) then rise to a point where a zigzag track leads steeply upwards. This is the old quarry track. As the gradient eases the path veers left to a cairn. Take the path which ascends rightwards in order to hug the summit ridge as best you can, for the most part, following along a stone wall. The rocky knoll of Brown Howe is reached and on its top a stile leads to the summit of Lingmoor.

The path descends along the side of a stone wall. This is crossed and the going steepens before abruptly emerging onto the gentle shoulder beneath Side Pike. A stile leads over to a narrow path which approaches the foot of the crag before squeezing left behind a rock flake. The path traverses left then ascends to the summit cone of Side Pike. Descend the ridge following the main path to join the road north of the cattle grid. Cross the road in front of the cattle grid, to take the path leading down to the delightful little wood behind Blea Tarn. Continue along the path to a footbridge crossing the stream on the left and follow the track through a kissing gate directly back to the car park.

BLAKE RIGG (LITTLE LANGDALE), 1755FT/535M; LONG CRAG on WRYNOSE FELL, 1788FT/545M; PIKE O'BLISCO, 2313FT/705M; GREAT KNOTT, 2283FT/696M; COLD PIKE, 2300FT/701M

Maps: OS OL6, L90: GR 285039, GR 280040, GR 272041, GR 260043, GR 263036
Access point: Wrynose Bridge, GR 285033
Distance/ascent: 5mls/2165ft, 8km/660m
Approx time: 3 hours

Above the bridge a vague path rises into the basin containing the finger-streams feeding the beck. Cross these to the right and traverse above Little Horse Crag onto the shoulder of Blake Rigg. Ascend its rocky top.

The plateau between here and the cairned rocky outcrop of Long Crag, the top of Wrynose Fell, is boggy but with prudence can be negotiated dry. There is no path. Best to descend Long Crag the same way as you ascended, then skirt around its northern end to gain access to the hollow beneath the slopes of Blisco. The ascent up grass, rock and scree leads to the rocky knoll of Blisco with its most northerly cairned top constituting the highest point of this excursion. A well-trodden path drops steeply towards Red Tarn. Cross the Browney Gill trod rising from Langdale and ascend gently towards The Crinkles. The slight domed rubble summit of Great Knott is reached by bearing right from the main trod as it levels. Contour around to the shoulder of Cold Pike and ascend to the summit – a crown of bare rock rising in a dignified manner above the grassy slopes below. The most northerly rocky outcrop is the highest point.

A good path, once the packhorse road track to the tarn, is

followed down to the Three Shires Stone. A short descent of the road completes the route.

GREAT KNOTT, 2283FT/696M; FIRST CRINKLE, 2733FT/833M; SECOND CRINKLE (LONG TOP), 2816FT/859M; THIRD CRINKLE, 2754FT/840M; FOURTH CRINKLE, 2730FT/832M; FIFTH CRINKLE (GUNSON KNOTT), 2674FT/815M; SHELTER CRAGS, 2674FT/815M; BOWFELL, 2960FT/902M; WHITE STONES on THE BAND, 1863FT/568M

Maps: OS OL6, L90: GR 260043, GR 250046, GR 248049, GR 250050, GR 250051, GR 250052, GR 250053, GR 261061
Access point: The Old Dungeon Ghyll Car Park, GR 286062
Distance/ascent: 8mls/3280ft, 13km/1000m
Approx time: 4¹/₂ hours

Proceed along the surfaced track to Stool End Farm beneath The Band. A gate beside the farmhouse gives access to the fell. Take the left track at the fork. Stiles lead over stone walls and a sheepfold is passed to the right before Oxendale beck is joined and a footbridge taken to cross it. Rise steeply, following stone steps and the constructed footpath over Brown Howe, to join the upper section of Browney Gill. It soon falls back to reveal the hollow, between Pike O'Blisco and Cold Pike, cradling Red Tarn. At the unmistakable junction of paths, bear right to rise again. Just off the path to the right Great Knott may be visited. The first all-rock outcrop, elongated and multi-cairned, is the First Crinkle. A dip is followed by the Bad Step, a short scramble neccessary, and ascent made to the cairn of Long Top – the second and highest Crinkle. For those who don't fancy the Bad Step an easy grassy rake can be found to the left (west) of the dip – this leads to the summit cairn.

TO CRINKLES AND BOWFELL

BOWFELL FROM ESKDALE

From Long Top, the main path bypasses the tops of the other Crinkles. Visiting them requires a detour. The conical Third Crinkle lies about 50 yards east above the path. The cairned Fourth Crinkle lies about ten yards east of the path, directly above steep cliffs. Gunson Knott, the Fifth Crinkle, a lower but distinctively-formed triangulated buttress of rock, is reached about 20m east of the path. The summit of Shelter Crags is crossed by the path which continues to descend to the col of the Three Tarns. Steep rocky scree leads to a level plateau beneath the the summit cone of Bowfell. Follow the path around the cone on its east before bearing back south taking the path to the summit.

Return to the Three Tarns and bear left down The Band. Where the path passes a little tarn and extensive peat bogs, a detour left leads to the summit of White Stones. There is no real path. Return to the main path traversing the flanks of White Stones – don't attempt to continue descending the crest of the ridge because a steep crag intervenes. A junction with the original course is reached at the toe of The Band.

HIGH GAIT CRAGS, 1877FT/572M; PIKE DE BIELD, 2657FT/810M; ESK PIKE, 2903FT/885M; BOWFELL, 2960FT/902M; SHELTER CRAGS, 2674FT/815M; FIFTH CRINKLE (GUNSON KNOTT), 2674FT/815M; FOURTH CRINKLE, 2703FT/832M; THIRD CRINKLE, 2754FT/840M; SECOND CRINKLE (LONG TOP), 2816FT/859M; FIRST CRINKLE, 2733FT/833M; STONESTY PIKE, 2510FT/765M; LITTLE STAND, 2428FT/740M

Maps: OS OL6, L90: GR 230058, GR 236068, GR 237075, GR 245065, GR 250053, GR 250052, GR 250051, GR 250050, GR 248049, GR 250046, GR 249041, GR 251034
Access point: Cockley Beck, GR 244018

Distance/ascent: 8¹/₂ mls/3345ft, 14km/1020m
Approx time: 5¹/₂ hours

Leave the road and follow a track along the bank above
Mosedale Beck. After the track enters the upper basin of
Mosedale and levels out, a path veers up to the left. Take this
and make a high circuitous traverse around the head of the basin.
Descend to and cross Lingcove Beck. Ascend right to Pianet
Knott. Skirt the rocky outcrops of Long Crag and Low Gait Crags
to make a beeline for High Gait Crags. The furthest bump, a
cairned rock outcrop, is the highest point.

Veer right to skirt the edge of Pike de Bield Moss and climb
the Ling Cove edge of the ridge. Above, a vague path can be picked
out moving left to skirt beneath a rocky outcrop. Immediately
above to the left, opposite the outcrop, is the separate thumb of
Pike de Bield and a little further the cairned accredited top.
Continue straight up the shoulder to the white summit rocks of Esk
Pike. Descend along the main path into Ore Gap. A long haul leads
to the summit of Bowell.

After skirting the top of the Great Slab to the left, the well-
defined footpath descends to the Three Tarns. The path across the
Crinkles is now reversed taking care descending the Bad Step.
Ater descending from the multi-cairned First Crinkle bear right to
strike a central line across the moss to Stonesty Pike. Beyond, a
rake descending beneath a long low wall of rock leads to the col
beneath Little Stand. A short climb leads to the summit.
A natural corridor descends from the summit rocks to reach a
terrace. Bear left to find the continuation of the corridor and
descend to a wire fence and stone wall. A stile leads to a path
through the bracken and into the valley bottom. A final stile and
footbridge or stepping stones lead back to the Hardknott road.

4 BORROWDALE FELLS

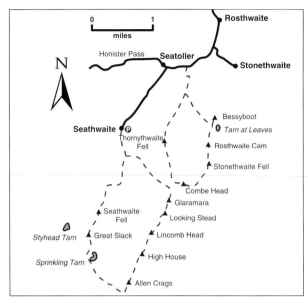

Location: Capping the head of Borrowdale near the centre of the Western Fells.

Suggested Bases: Keswick and Borrowdale.

Accommodation: Keswick: all facilities except railway station; Longthwaite youth hostel; camping at The Headlands (Derwent Water), Castlerigg Hall and Castlerigg Farm. *Borrowdale:* Barrow House youth hostel; b&b at The Scafell Inn; camping at Ashness Farm, Dalt Wood-Grange, Stonethwaite, Thornythwaite and Seathwaite farms. Bus service from Keswick.

THORNYTHWAITE FELL, 1883FT/574M; COMBE HEAD, 2405FT/733M; STONETHWAITE FELL, 2073FT/632M; ROSTHWAITE CAM on ROSTHWAITE FELL, 2008FT/612M; BESSYBOOT on ROSTHWAITE FELL, 1807FT/550M

Maps: OS OL4, L90: GR 245118, GR 250109, GR 256114, GR 256118, GR 258125

Access point: Immediately below Strands Bridge on the Borrowdale Road, opposite the cottages of Mountain View, a narrow road leads to Thornythwaite. Follow this for approximately 400 metres to parking on the right, GR 249135

Distance/ascent: 5mls/2395ft, 8km/730m
Approx time: 3¹/₂ hours

Along the road, in the direction of Strands Bridge, a gate/stile gives access to the wooded field on the right. A track leads directly to the path (the path itself begins at another stile placed nearer Strands Bridge) which sweeps rightwards through the woods to a kissing gate in a stone wall. The path splits: take the right fork. Initially it rises steeply taking a sharp rib but soon the gradient slackens and the path ambles onto the shoulder of Thornythwaite Fell. The summit of Thornythwaite Fell is a blocky rock knoll standing above the path and protruding only slightly from the general run of the shoulder.

The path continues across a rift, passing an area where the rocks resemble a spewn heap of paving stones. At this point it bears right aiming for Glaramara. We however quit it left to take rougher and steeper ground rising to Combe Head. There is no real path. Descend slightly right of the edge taking a line into the great natural corridor of the Combe Door. Contour around the rocky outcrop forming the eastern 'doorpost' to find an indistinct path leading to the hollow below. On the far side take a grassy break rising up the rocky bump and over a stone wall. The vague path bears right over the shoulder but first climb up left to the largest top overlooking The Combe – the summit of Stonethwaite Fell.

Bear right and descend to Great Hollow, taking the vague path on its right side. On leaving the hollow the cubic block summit of Rosthwaite Cam lies to the left. Descend by the same route and continue to traverse the flanks above the delightfully named Tarn at Leaves. Don't miss the nose of Bessyboot, cairned with a well-worn path. Retrace your steps down the nose before heading straight towards The Combe. Cross the beck and join your original route.

SEATHWAITE FELL, 1970FT/601M; GREAT SLACK on SEATHWAITE FELL, 2073FT/632M; ALLEN CRAGS, 2574FT/785M; HIGH HOUSE on ALLEN CRAGS, 2244FT/684M; LINCOMB HEAD on GLARAMARA, 2365FT/721M; LOOKING STEAD on GLARAMARA, 2543FT/775M; GLARAMARA, 25658FT/783M

Maps: OS OL4, OL6, L90: GR 229102, GR 227097, GR 237086, GR 240093, GR 243097, GR 246102, GR 246105
Access point: The head of the Seathwaite valley, by the side of the road beneath the farm – don't block any field entrances or use the road, GR 236123
Distance/ascent: 7mls/2950ft, 11km/900m
Approx time: 4¹/₂ hours

Walk through the farm and follow the track over Stockley Bridge, before rising up the fell away from Grains Gill. The path continues through a gate in the fell wall after which the

OVER SEATHWAITE FELL TO THE GABLES

old packhorse route will be found to bear left (the modern path to Styhead bears right). Follow this until it is necessary to move left again past the end of Black Waugh. Aim for the right of Aaron Crags to find a gully. Although this is steep, it is grassy in nature and quite straightforward. Pass a tumbled wall on a rocky nose above the crag to reach the cairned summit of Seathwaite Fell, a rocky knoll standing just above a little tarn.

Take the tarn and the next in anticlockwise manner, until a cylindrical cairn stands above a third tarn. Numerous little tarns follow before the rocky top of Great Slack. Finally a larger (unnamed on the OS map) tarn is passed followed by Sprinkling Tarn before the main trod is reached. Bear left and ascend to Esk Hause, thereafter branching left to the summit of Allen Crags. A rough broad ridge falls easily to the gap holding High House and Lincomb Tarns. A detour from the well-blazoned path is necessary to reach the little rocky knoll of High House above.

Beyond the two tarns the shoulder climbs to Glaramara; the main path traversing to the right of its most northerly top, Lincomb Head. Move back up and left to reach it. Next to be ascended, lying dead ahead, is the middle top of Glaramara – Looking Steads. Two rocky points rise above the summit; the north-easterly of these is the summit of Glaramara.

Descend to move right across the summit plateau. Scramble down a steep well-worn rocky runnel which leads down through the craggy north face that crowns the fell. Easier boggy ground follows before a line of cairns can be seen leading away to the left. Follow them until the head of Hind Gill can be identified. Take the left bank in descent. At its base the open fellside levels before a gate through the stone wall leads easily down towards the main track traversing the valley floor.

5 ESKDALE FELLS

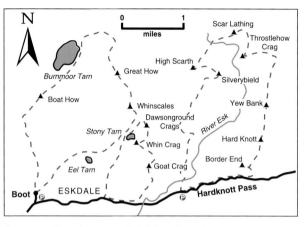

Location: Encircling upper Eskdale and north of the Eskdale Valley, Western Fells.

Suggested Bases: Eskdale.

Accommodation: *Eskdale:* self-catering accommodation and b&b at The Burnmoor and The Woolpack Inns; Eskdale youth hostel; camping at Boot, Fisherground Farm.

BORDER END, 1713FT/522M; HARD KNOTT, 1803FT/549M; YEW BANK, 1637FT/499M; THROSTLEHOW CRAG, 1325FT/404M; SCAR LATHING, 1440FT/439M; HIGH SCARTH, 1598FT/487M; SILVERYBIELD, 1296FT/395M

Maps: OS OL6, L90: GR 229018, GR 232023, GR 232031, GR 227044, GR 226050, GR 215044, GR 222039

Access point: Top of Hardknott Pass, GR 232015

Return point: Brotherilkeld by the telephone kiosk, GR 211011

Distance/ascent: 7½ mls/1575ft; 11.5km/480m

Approx time: 5 hours

Below the summit of the pass on the east a path leads up a natural grass rake to a boggy hollow in the ridge above. Bear left, rising to a cairned rocky outcrop. Continue to the next upstanding area on the edge overlooking Eskdale, the OS accredited summit of Border End. Return to the hollow and strike north following cairns to rise slightly, then pass through the large knots of rock on the shoulder. In front lies the biggest of the rock pyramids and the summit cairn of Hard Knott.

Descend heading due north with a mountain tarn (unnamed on OS) to your right; on the left the craggy top of Yew Bank. Continue easily down the grassy highway to the top of Mosedale and then down to Lingcove Beck. Boulder-hopping gives a dry crossing and above a path contours left. When it begins to ascend, leave it to continue the traverse left across a boggy section. An old broken stone wall rises up the hillside towards the grassy dome summit of Throstlehow Crag.

Head north descending to cross the path and pass to the right of the bog beyond. Rise steeply to the grassy neck leading to the top of Scar Lathing. Descend to the west. There is a large boulder on the opposite bank of the River Esk: make a beeline for this, crossing just above the rocky rapids (in spate a crossing will be impossible). Cross the main footpath and continue to rise, bearing left to the vague summit of High Scarth Crag.

Circumnavigate a rocky knoll to the left, where a grassed corridor leads down to the main track. Cross it and pass the bog to the left beneath some little crags. Then rise to the rocky knott of Silverybield. Go round the southern end of Silverybield bog to return to the main path. Follow this until a good track zigzags down to the valley floor reaching Scale Bridge before running down left through the fields to Taw House Farm. A wooden stile leads to a corridor down the edge of the field and a wooden footbridge across the River Esk. The track skirts Brotherilkeld Farm and continues to the road and telephone kiosk.

DAWSONGROUND CRAGS, 1302FT/397M; WHIN CRAG (ESKDALE), 1158FT/353M; GOAT CRAG, 1024FT/312M

Maps: OS OL6, L90: GR 204027, GR 200023, GR 204018
Access point: Car park right of the Woolpack Inn, GR 190010
Distance/ascent: 3¾ mls/1200ft, 6km/365m
Approx time: 2 hours

Rounding the left end of the building and taking a small gate behind, the track rises from the Woolpack Inn. The larch plantation is exited by another small gate. Continue along the track, ignore the fork left and go straight ahead into the rocky hummocks. Again ignore a track swinging off left, invisible in any case when the bracken grows high. Peelplace Noddle is traversed before an ascent is made to the left. Cross a stream and make a final pull to gain the shoulder. Secluded Stony Tarn lies to the right with its cirque of heathery crags above.

Skirt the end of the tarn, recrossing the stream, before rising up left to a ruined building. Contour right under a craggy outcrop and climb to the heathery plateau. Bear right to find the top of Dawsonground Crags. Follow the ridge running out above the tarn. The cairned top at its end is the summit of Whin Crag. Pick a careful line back east heading for the light granite dome of Goat Crag. Descend through craggy outcrops, to a grassy hollow and cross this over bog and stream, to pass the granite cliff of Bull How. Ascend to the gain the top of Goat Crag, crossing a peaty hollow just below the summit.

Below the summit a natural narrow corridor leads between the rocks before a traverse right, beneath a steep slabby wall, leads easily down to a well-defined path (a popular route from Wha House to the Slight Side shoulder of Scafell). Follow this to the road and in turn to the Woolpack Inn.

BOAT HOW, 1105FT/337M; GREAT HOW on ESKDALE FELL, 1713FT/522M; WHINSCALES on ESKDALE FELL, 1394FT/425M

Maps: OS OL6, L90: GR 177034, GR 198040, GR 197033
Access point: Boot, GR 176011. Car park at The Burnmoor Inn.
Ask permission from the landlord. Do not park and walk.
Distance/ascent: 7mls/1800ft, 11km/550m
Approx time: 3¹/₂ hours

Our way lies over the stone-arched bridge, past the mill and onto the stone-walled bridleway leading in the direction of Brat's Moss. Zigzagging steeply at first the bridleway is lined with walls constructed from hefty boulders of Eskdale Granite. As open moor is encountered, a cluster of interesting old stone buildings – Peat Houses – are passed. In front of the last building the track bears right, up onto Brat's Moss. As the track levels to cross Brat's Hill a grassed bump stands to the left. Leave the track to surmount this to find, immediately below on the other side, a stone circle; beyond this are another two circles. Pass these and climb onto the shoulder of Low Longrigg to discover two smaller circles. Ascend the easy grassy shoulder towards the rocky knoll summit of Boat How.

An easy descent leads down the broad spur to Burnmoor Tarn. The path crosses a bridge over Whillan Beck before the track bears right across the bog. Cross the stream, no problem in normal conditions, just above the confluence of Hardrigg and Oliver Gills. Ascend the steep rough hillside directly above to find a hidden path that has traversed the hillside from distant Lambford Bridge. Continue along the path to the side of Oliver Gill. Follow the gill up until it enters a little ravine, cutting through the end of Bleaberry How. Keep to the south bank (no real path) traversing its steep sides. After a little way it is better to climb out right, up the northern shoulder rising to the rocky summit of Eskdale Fell – Great How. A cleft in the rocks will be found to the west. Descend through this to find a crescent-shaped spur leading to the top of Whinscales. The shoulder continues to fall towards Stony Tarn. It then bears right. Intermittent paths disappear and reappear but with care you can descend to Eel Tarn.

The path leads above the north shore to a good track. Follow the track through a corridor formed by stone walls taking the signed 'Bridleway To Boot'.

6 THE SCAFELLS

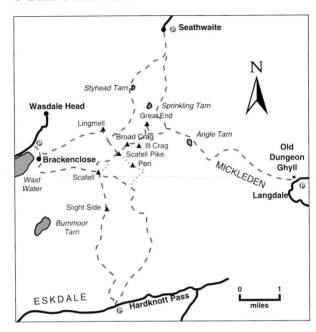

Location: Looking down over the heads of Wasdale, Borrowdale, Eskdale and distant Great Langdale, Western Fells.

Suggested Bases: Wasdale, Borrowdale, Great Langdale and Eskdale.

Accommodation: Wasdale: self catering and b&b at Wasdale Head, The Wasdale Head Inn, Wasdale Hall youth hostel; camping at Wasdale Head. *Borrowdale:* youth hostels at Longthwaite and Barrow House. B&B at The Scafell Inn; camping at Ashness Farm, Dalt Wood-Grange, Stonethwaite, Thornythwaite and Seathwaite farms. Bus service from Keswick. *Great Langdale:* self-catering accommodation and b&b; The Old Dungeon Ghyll and Stickle Barn Inns (the latter with bunkhouse); Elterwater and Langdale (High Close) youth hostels; camping at head of Great Langdale, Baysbrown Farm, Neaum Crag above Skelwith Bridge; bus service from Ambleside to the Old Dungeon Ghyll. *Eskdale:* self-catering accomodation and b&b at The Burnmoor and The Woolpack Inns; Eskdale youth hostel; camping at Boot, Fisherground Farm.

GREAT END, 2985FT/910M; ILL CRAG (SCAFELL), 3067FT/935M; BROAD CRAG, 3054FT/931M; SCAFELL PIKE, 3210FT/978M

Maps: OS OL6, L90: GR 226084, GR 223074, GR 219076, GR 216072
Access point: Old Dungeon Ghyll Hotel Car Park, GR 286062
Distance/ascent: 11mls/3775ft, 18km/1150m
Approx time: 7 hours

From the Old Dungeon Ghyll the walled stony track soon gives way to the openness of Mickleden. Rosset Gill presents the first steep climb. Alternatively an old packhorse track zigzags more sedately upwards on its left, joining the gill at its head. The demanding ascent is worthwhile because a little way in front lies Angle Tarn, nestling in a secluded hollow beneath Hanging Knotts. The gentle ascent from the tarn leads to the stony shoulder of Esk Hause and the stone-walled shelter which is formed in a cross. Proceed along the stone path until it is possible to move rightwards to the broad summit of Great End. A cairn and trig point stand amidst a sprawl of rocks.

The shoulder descends at first then rises and you should bear left off the main path to gain the peak of Ill Crag. Latest OS data puts this as the second in altitude to the Scafell Pikes. Descend to the main path situated in a deep gap below the rocky shoulder of Broad Crag. The main path rises to pass the top of Broad Crag on its southern flank before dropping to the gap beneath Scafell Pike. To reach the summit of Broad Crag, bear right at the highest point and make a rough scramble over awkward boulder and scree.

Return to the main path and descend into the gap ahead. Rise steeply up the other side. Soon your effort will be rewarded; the angle slackens and the path leads easily over the summit dome to a large circular chambered cairn – the top of Scafell Pike. Return to Langdale on the main well-defined path which takes a central route beneath the tops of Broad Crag and Ill Crag to Esk Hause, without taking in Great End.

SCAFELL, 3162FT/964M; SLIGHT SIDE, 2499FT/762M

Maps: OS OL6, L90: GR 207065, GR 210050
Access point: Car park by the side of the Hardknott Pass just above the cattle grid at Brotherilkeld, GR 214011
Distance/ascent: 8¼ mls/2950ft, 13.5km/900m
Approx time: 5 hours

Find the path running above the plantation to enter the fields above Brotherilkeld Farm. The well-defined path leads into upper Eskdale. Cross over Lingcove Bridge and begin climbing towards Great Moss. The path flattens, passes beneath Scar Lathing, and continues to follow the true left bank of the River Esk. The bog here is known as Great Moss. To the left, How Beck makes an impressive waterfall and a valley leads up to Mickledore. Above the confluence, where How Beck joins the Esk, make a crossing. Take the steep path rising impressively just right of the waterfall – scrambling may be necessary. Continue up the steep hanging valley above until, some 100 metres below the rocky bastion of the East Buttress, a stream issues from a stony gully to the left.

Climb the gully, rough but not difficult which leads directly to Fox's Tarn. The smallest tarn in the Lake District. (Note: if the gully is missed a well-defined traverse takes a higher route to the tarn). The way lies directly up to the shoulder, then left to find the summit cairn of Scafell, situated on a slight rise. The remains of a ruined shelter lie just beyond. Descend the long shoulder over Long Green and on to Slight Side. The summit cairn lies on top of the sloping rock outcrop (also called Horn Crag). A rough scramble leads through the rocks down to the right; the path leads down the flanks of Scafell. Rapid progress can be made until the going levels to cross the upper rim of Cowcove before crossing Cat Cove Beck. Beyond the ravine running below Cat Crags, our path breaks down to the left (straight on leads to the road above Wha House farm). Weave a way down the hillside to the track by the gate in the wall. Take the lower gate into the field and continue to Taw House farm. A stile leads left to a corridor formed by stone wall, post and wire fence leading to the footbridge over the River Esk. The path skirts Brotherilkeld farm to join the road at the foot of Hardknott Pass by the telephone kiosk.

PEN, 2500FT/762M; SCAFELL PIKE, 3210FT/978M; SCAFELL, 3162FT/964M

Maps: OS OL6, L90: GR 221068, GR 216072
Access point: As per previous route, GR 214011.
Distance/ascent: 10³/₄ mls/3325ft, 17.5km/1015m
Approx time: 6¹/₄ hours

This route involves exposed scrambling while ascending to Pen and easy exposed rock climbing on the ascent of Broad Stand. Follow the previous route to cross the River Esk approaching the waterfall of How Beck then bear right – a high line avoids most of the boggy ground to cross beneath Esk Buttress (named Dow Crag and Central Pillar on the OS maps). Continue beneath a lesser crag with a prominent gash up its front – this is Thor's Buttress. Follow a vague path rising into Little Narrowcove but quickly move off left into a broad easy gully. Continue left to tackle the rocky pyramid summit of Pen by its left side.

After descending continue up the broad ridge beyond, taking the rocky wall on its left to make a rough bouldery ascent. When the angle eases the cairned rocky knoll to the left is the Eskdale Cairn. Cross the rocky plateau beyond to the summit of Scafell Pike. An easy path makes a stony descent to the start of the Mickledore edge connecting Scafell Pike to Scafell. A path falls left to traverse beneath the rocks of the East Buttress. A short way

THE SCAFELLS FROM RED PIKE

down this a narrow cleft in the rock, formed by a large block, provides the narrow squeeze access to Broad Stand. The bottom section comprisies of a series of stepped walls, individually some 5m in height. The ground falls rapidly away to the left and exposure is considerable.

Wriggle through the cleft rising to a rock ledge beneath the first wall. Step left on very polished rock. Climb up and right to a ledge beneath the second wall. Climb the second wall directly or by the corner (technically the most difficult section) – in either case only a few feet need be made before a good handhold can be taken on the ledge above. Slabby rocks lead out rightwards to easier angled ground where it is again possible to assume a standing position.

The path continues up then left through a notch in the rocks to the easy top section of a gully (Mickledore Gully – a graded rock climb which offers no easy way below). Note loose rocks and scree abound and it is imperative that nothing is dislodged for rock climbers may be on the cliffs below. Continue up the gully until it is possible to bear left along the rocky top. Continue to the path above Fox's Tarn and proceed along the broad shoulder plateau leading to the summit of Scafell. Descend as per the previous route.

LINGMELL (WASDALE), 2649FT/807M; SCAFELL PIKE, 3210FT/978M; SCAFELL, 3162FT/964M

Maps: OS OL6, L90: GR 209082, GR 216072, GR 207065
Access point: Car park, alongside camp site at the head of
    Wast Water, GR 182074
Distance/ascent: 6¹/₄ mls/3840ft, 10km/1170m
Approx time: 5 hours

After crossing the concrete bridge turn left to follow the stream bank, passing Brackenclose on the right. Cross a wooden footbridge and take the path rising with Lingmell Gill. Beyond a fence a path bears off left to the shoulder of Lingmell. (Straight on leads up Brown Tongue to Hollow Stones and then via steep scree directly to Mickledore, the shortest route and a hard slog. Useful to the walker as a safe and quick descent from Mickledore). Although initially the going is steep, above the 1800ft/550m contour the angle recedes and pleasant walking leads to the left of Goat Crags and to the summit of Lingmell. Descend the grassy slope over a ruined stone wall into the hollow of Lingmell Col (junction with The Corridor Route from Sty Head). The well-defined path rises to the right before sweeping back left over the rocky plateau to the summit cairn of Scafell Pike.

From the cairn a well-worn path makes a rocky descent to the ridge of Mickledore. Nearing the Scafell end of Mickledore a scree slope – steep, rough going so care must be exercised – leads down to a long ledge traversing beneath the north facing precipice of Scafell Crag. At the end of this, Lord's Rake, running in the same line as the ledge, cuts upwards through the rocks.

Scree has been eroded to leave bare sections of rock and the ascent should be treated with caution. The rake contains three ups and two downs all continuing in a straight line to the open fell. A path leads up left onto the shoulder and in turn the summit of Scafell.

From the summit a vague path leads easily and quickly down the grass flanks of the mountain, over Green How, to join the track above Fence Wood and Wasdale Head Hall farm. Bear right through the sweet oaks of Brackenclose to Lingmell Gill.

SCAFELL PIKE, 3210FT/978M; BROAD CRAG, 3054FT/931M; ILL CRAG (SCAFELL), 3067FT/935M; GREAT END, 2984FT/910M

Maps: OS OL4, OL6, L90: GR 216072, GR 219076, GR 223074, GR 226084

Access point: Head of Seathwaite Valley, Borrowdale. Be early because it gets crowded. Don't block any field entrances or the road, GR 236123

Distance/ascent: 8½ mls/3350ft, 14km/1020m

Approx time: 5 hours

The track through the farm leads easily to Stockley Bridge across Grains Gill. The track leads up through the gate in the fell wall and bears right to sweep up the shoulder above the larches of Taylorgill Force. The ascent eases and follows Styhead Gill to cross it by a wooden footbridge before traversing the banks of Styhead Tarn. Sty Head lies just beyond the tarn and this route rises up the shoulder of the col to the left. After a brief ascent a slight descent is made to the right to the start of the Corridor Route beneath Spout Head. The path follows a natural course through rugged and exposed ground. The Corridor ends just above

SCAFELL ABOVE WAST WATER

Lingmell Col from where the path leads directly up the stony slopes of Scafell Pike. It bears right then back left to cross the summit plateau and reach the large cairn.

Heading north east across the plateau the path falls to the col beneath Scafell Pike and Broad Crag. Follow the main path along the northen spine, with diversions first left and then right to include the tops of Broad Crag and Ill Crag, to the summit cairn of Great End. From here retrace your steps before a course can be followed to the path descending to Esk Hause. A cairn marks the junction of routes, Esk Pike to the right, Esk Hause Shelter straight down. Continue down to the shelter, then bear left along the main track under Great End. The stream on the right is crossed and a well-defined path taken down to the right of Ruddy Gill. A recently constructed footpath leads down to a bridge crossing Grains Gill. The path leads down the left bank of the gill to Stockley Bridge.

7 THE SCREES

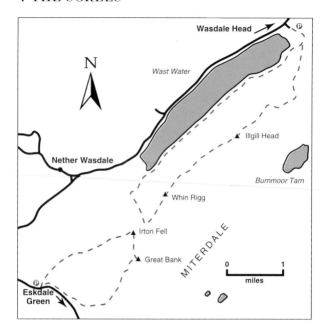

Location: Extending above the south-eastern shore of Wast Water,
   Western Fells.
Suggested Bases: Wasdale and Nether Wasdale.
Accommodation: Wasdale: self-catering and b&b at Wasdale Head,
   The Wasdale Head Inn, Wasdale Hall youth hostel; camping
   at Wasdale Head. *Nether Wasdale:* self-catering and b&b;
   The Strands and The Screes Inns; camping.

IRTON FELL, 1296FT/395M; GREAT BANK, 1079FT/329M

Maps: OS OL6, L89: GR 144026, GR 144019
Access point: Old quarry car park by the side of the Eskdale
   Bridge to Santon Bridge Road, GR 121012
Distance/ascent: 4¼ mls/1065ft, 7km/325m
Approx time: 2 hours

 By the side of the quarry, in the direction of Santon Bridge, a
signs reads 'Public Footpath Wasdale Head'. Rising above the
quarry, through the forestry, the path reaches a forest track.

THE SCREES TUMBLING FROM ILLGILL HEAD INTO WAST WATER

Follow this, bearing right at a junction. The track leads above a
stone wall to exit the forest via a stile next to a gate. Numerous
piles of stones lie mainly to the left. The path continues easily along
the grassy shoulder by the stone wall, with afforested Miterdale
lying to the right.

A stile leads over a wall until finally the shoulder levels. Bear
right to the grassy summit bumps of Irton Fell. The most north-
easterly being the highest. Either continue along the top to pick up
the line of an old wall at the head of Greathall Gill or descend
directly towards Great Bank. In either case the wall skirts forest to
form a distinct corner from which point access is made to Great
Bank.

Stride the post and wire fence. At this point there is a clearing
in the forest. Climb up through thick tussocks of grass and heather
to the summit. Cross a ruined stone wall to the top. Return to the
neck and descend by the stone wall until a point at which it
disappears into the forest. Bear left, through rough heather and
boulders, to a break in the conifers below. Descend to this and
continue in the same line through the trees. Find a gap in a stone
wall with Merebeck Gill on the far side. A vague path leads down
the bank to enter a group of larches. On the left an open stone
gateway leads through the wall. Descend through the woods to
reach a forestry track and bear right along this.

The track leads easily through the forest. Ignore the first
branch to the right and, shortly afterwards, the bridleway crossing
it. Continue straight along the track at the next junction, finally
descending Crabtree Dale Wood to briefly emerge into open
territory. Keyhow Coppice follows before the drive to Cubbens is
reached and shortly afterwards the road.

3

ILLGILL HEAD, 1998FT/609M; WHIN RIGG (WASDALE), 1755FT/535M

Maps: OS OL6, L89: GR 169049, GR 152034
Access point: Car park, alongside the camp site, at the head of
   Wast Water, GR 182074
Distance/ascent: 8¼ mls/2020ft, 13.5km/615m
Approx time: 4½ hours

The track leads over a concrete bridge after which a left turn
is made following the bank of the stream. Skirt right through
the oaks beneath Brackenclose and find a path emerging from
the far corner of its grounds. This rises through Fence Wood to
emerge onto the fell beneath the col. An old wall points up the
shoulder of Illgill Head and the path leads directly to a group of
stones and, according to the latest OS information, the rather non-
descript summit. The trig point and cairn lie just beyond nearer
the rim of the screes. The main path along the crest between Illgill
Head and Whin Rigg traverses rolling grassland with the summit
cairn placed close to the edge of The Screes.

Easy descent down the western shoulder leads towards the top
of the ravine of Greathall Gill. A path bears right to pick a course
over steep ground down the right flank of the gill. Below the base
of the ravine follow the line of a stone wall to the right which leads
to a track above the lake shore. Continue along this passing the
pump house. A path traverses the screes above the shore of Wast
Water.

At first the path is well-defined and quite straightforward, but
then deteriorates to present a degree of strenuous boulder-
hopping. The path again takes shape and crosses brackened
hillside to pick up the track leading past Wasdale Head Hall Farm.

8 GREAT GABLE GROUP

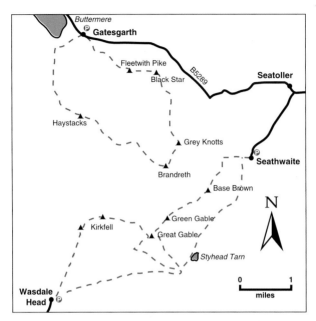

Location: Found at the heads of Buttermere, Borrowdale and
   Wasdale in the heart of the Western Fells.
Suggested Bases: Buttermere, Borrowdale and Wasdale Head.
Accomodation: Buttermere: self-catering accommodation and b&b,
   The Fish Inn, Honister Hause and Buttermere youth hostels;
   camping at Gatesgarth Farm. *Borrowdale:* Barrow House
   youth hostel; b&b at The Scafell Inn; camping at Ashness
   Farm, Dalt Wood-Grange, Stonethwaite, Thornythwaite and
   Seathwaite farms. Bus service from Keswick. *Wasdale:* self-
   catering and b&b at Wasdale Head, The Wasdale Head Inn,
   Wasdale Hall youth hostel; camping at Wasdale Head.

FLEETWITH PIKE, 2126FT/648M; BLACK STAR on HONISTER CRAG,
2077FT/633M; GREY KNOTTS, 2287FT/697M; BRANDRETH, 2344FT/715M;
HAYSTACKS, 1959FT/597M

Maps: OS OL4, L90: GR 206141, GR 213141, GR 219126,
   GR 215119, GR 193132
Access point: Car park by Gatesgarth Farm, Buttermere. A small
   fee is payable at the farm, GR 195150

Distance/ascent: 6¼ mls/2790ft; 10km/850m
Approx time: 4 hours

A path rises steeply up Fleetwith Edge giving straightforward ascent to the top of Fleetwith Pike. Continue across the top to reach Black Star, the top of Honister Crag. The path descends down the shoulder through the slate workings and then over the raised bank of the dismantled tramway to join the main path that has risen from Honister Pass. Keep on the path until it stretches beneath the flanks of Grey Knotts. Bear left up the grassy hillside with a broken crag to your left. There is a trig point and just west, with a better view, a cairned rock outcrop. Both are of equal altitude. Follow the line of old iron fence posts to Brandreth. A straightforward descent leads to the left of the craggy plug of Great Round How and down to the waters of Blackbeck Tarn. Bear left at its head to roughly traverse a rock outcrop. Climb to a corridor through the heather which leads to a well-defined path passing Innominate Tarn on the left.

The path rises to crest a rocky ridge running across it. Cairned at either end it is the north point which is usually taken as the summit of Haystacks. Beyond to the west lies another shallow tarn, the Summit Tarn. Pass this before a rocky descent leads to Scarth Gap. The rough track forming Scarth Gap Pass, the old packhorse road between Buttermere and Ennerdale, is followed down the flanks of Buttermere Fell beneath High Crag to cross the bridge over Warnscale Beck and return over the meadows to Gatesgarth Farm.

BASE BROWN, 2120FT/646M; GREEN GABLE, 2628FT/801M; GREAT GABLE, 2949FT/899M

Maps: OS OL4, L90: GR 225115, GR 215107, GR 211103
Access point: Head of the Seathwaite Valley, Borrowdale. Do not block any field entrances or the road, GR 236123
Distance/ascent: 5mls/2855ft;8km/870m
Approx time: 4 hours

From the farmyard turn right under the arch. Take the footpath across the field to the footbridge which crosses the beck above its confluence with Sourmilk Gill. The path follows the left side of the gill rising into the empty combe with Gillercombe Buttress ahead (this is the climber's name for the crag, on OS maps it is named Raven Crag). Rising to flank the slopes of Base Brown a large balanced boulder is visible on the skyline to the left. Bear left off the path at this point (no obvious path) to rise diagonally to the craggy end known as Hanging Stone. Below the crag is a huge fallen block and balanced on top of the crag another great block taking the distinctive shape of a gladiator's helmet. Pass left beneath the crag, with no difficulty despite initial appearances. Find a good path ascending the shoulder directly to the cairned grassy summit of Base Brown.

GREAT GABLE ABOVE WASDALE HEAD

Descend easily to the grassy col of Blackmoor Pols. Join the main path rising from Gillercombe. Follow this directly to the stony summit of Green Gable. Drop to Windy Gap and climb steeply up rock and scree to cross the summit plateau and reach the summit rocks of Great Gable. A well-worn path heads off to Sty Head descending the broad south eastern edge of the mountain. Bear left to take the path past Styhead Tarn and continue along the left side of Styhead Gill. This drops to skirt the Scots Pine and Larch surrounding Taylorgill Force. A little rocky scramble (straightforward) leads to a short wall and gate to the side of the waterfall. The path continues below bearing left away from the river to make a gradual descent. Eventually the footbridge beneath Sourmilk Gill is re-crossed and retreat made through the arch into the farmyard.

GREAT GABLE, 2949FT/899M; NORTH TOP of KIRK FELL, 2582FT/787M; KIRK FELL, 2630FT/802M

Maps: OS OL 4, OL 6, L 90: GR 211103, GR 199107, GR 195105
Access point: Car park at Wasdale Head Inn, GR 187088; or from Wasdale Green where the track leads off the road to the church.
Distance/ascent: 6³/₄ mls/2640ft; 11km/1110m
Approx time: 4¹/₂ hours

From the car park outside the Wasdale Head Inn cross the fields past the tiny Wasdale Church and join the track. Beyond the buildings the final meadows are crossed before the valley narrows.

A footbridge leads over Gable Beck. Soon the track begins to rise up the fell and scree to Sty Head. Follow the main path up the north-east edge of Gable for only a little way before it branches off left to traverse beneath the cleanly cut cliff of Kern Knotts. This route is known as the Climber's Traverse and involves a little easy scrambling. Rising slightly the path traverses the hillside crossing an extensive area of scree. The path levels, crossing the head of a scree slope. It then intercepts the steep scree and boulder-filled runnel of Great Hell Gate. Continue to traverse beneath the rocky crags of The Napes until the path splits. The lower path leads easily across to the next fan of scree – Little Hell Gate. The most interesting route is to take the higher path which rises up a gully on the left side of Napes Needle. Make a rocky traverse left beneath the cliff to a narrow squeeze behind a great block. Climbing down from this squeeze into the gully beyond constitutes the most technically difficult section.

Pass under the distinctive Sphinx rock to reach Little Hell Gate just around the corner. A vague path leads up the right side of the scree corridor. It is steep going as far as Westmorland Crags. Here the path bears left to rise up the final section of bouldery scree to the summit of Great Gable. Alternatively climb the gully immediately right of the Sphinx to find a broken path near the ridge marking Little Hell Gate – thus avoiding the tiresome scree ascent.

Take the path leading down the north-western shoulder of the mountain. Cross Moses' Trod and continue over the col of Beck Head to climb Rib End following the path to the cairn marking the north top of Kirk Fell. The higher summit of Kirk Fell lies beyond the two little tarns, collectively known as Kirkfell Tarn. A steep, though easy path falls directly down the nose to the valley floor.

9 PILLAR GROUP

Location: Between the valleys of Wasdale and Ennerdale, Western Fells.

Suggested Bases: Wasdale and Ennerdale

Accommodation: Wasdale: self catering and b&b at Wasdale Head, The Wasdale Head Inn, Wasdale Hall youth hostel; camping at Wasdale Head. *Ennerdale:* b&b; Ennerdale Bridge Inn, High Gillerthwaite and Black Sail youth hostels; no camping.

LOOKING STEAD, 2057FT/627M; PILLAR, 2927FT/892M; BLACK CRAG (PILLAR), 2717FT/828M; SCOAT FELL, 2760FT/841M; STEEPLE, 2687FT/819M; RED PIKE, 2709FT/826M

Maps: OS OL4, OL6, L89: GR 186118, GR 171121, GR 166116, GR 160114, GR 157117, GR 165106

Access point: Car park at Wasdale Head Inn, GR 187088

Distance/ascent: 7mls/3430ft, 11.5km/1045m

Approx time: 4³/₄ hours

![walker icon] Gain the path along the bank of Mosedale Beck running behind the Wasdale Head Inn. Turn left through the gate marked 'Black Sail Pass' and enter the remote vale of Mosedale. Continue to bear right and ascend Black Sail Pass. Once on the shoulder it is worth bearing right to the top of Looking Stead. A small cairn situated on a rock outcrop beyond the old iron fence posts. Follow the main path ascending the shoulder. The summit and trig point of Pillar reveal the rounded head of the mountain.

An easy descent is made to Wind Gap before rising to the bouldery summit cairn of Black Crag. Continue to the col above Mirk Cove then follow the northern edge of the wall to Scoat Fell. Divided into two tops, Little and Great Scoat Fell on the OS map, the actual summit of Scoat Fell is rather indefinite and found beside the highest section the stone wall. Below to the right, rising from the shoulder, lies the rocky tower of Steeple. After climbing this, re-ascend the shoulder of Scoat Fell to continue along the Mosedale Horseshoe.

Descend the flanks of Scoat Fell to gain the shoulder of Red Pike. The path leads to a cairn midway along the shoulder – this isn't the summit. The cairn beyond and to the left, perched on the edge of the shoulder marks the summit. The path descends the northern edge of the hill, through boulder and rock outcrops without difficulty to reach the col of Dore Head. Our way lies to the left, down Dorehead Screes and Mosedale. Steep and eroded, it is best to descend the hillside to the left (north) initially, before traversing into the scree shoot. Cross it and follow its southern side until the angle eases and it can be followed to the floor of the vale. The path leads down Mosedale to join the beck and crosses over the packhorse bridge just before the Wasdale Head Inn.

PILLAR ROCK, 2560FT/780M; PILLAR, 2927FT/892M

Maps: OS OL4, OL6, L89: GR 172124, GR 171121
Access point: Car park at Wasdale Head Inn, GR 187088
Distance/ascent: 7mls/3600ft, 11.5km/1095m
Approx time: 6½ hours

![walker icon] The top of Pillar Rock can only be reached by rock climbing. Follow the previous route to Looking Stead. Just beyond the summit, marked by a small cairn, a narrow path breaks off from the shoulder to traverse the Ennerdale flank of Pillar Mountain, the high-level route. Make an exposed traverse across the hillside to gain a broad bouldery rake leading to a shoulder and Robinson's Cairn. Descend slightly from the cairn to cross a rocky hollow and ascend a minor rock ridge. A short section of scree gives access to a rake which rises diagonally rightwards through the crag – The Shamrock Traverse. This is well-defined but exposed. At the end of the rake there is a scree-filled gully down to the right called East Jordan Gully. Do not attempt to descend this. At its head is Jordan Gap which separates Pisgah, the rocky buttress on the left adjoining the hillside, from the summit of Pillar Rock.

At a suitable point traverse rightwards from the main path descending into East Jordan Gully. The route now described is known as 'The Slab And Notch Climb' and involves 200ft/65m of rock climbing. It is classed as 'moderately difficult' and usually tackled when roped up. Seen from across the gully a large light-coloured slab of rock leads to a higher smaller slab with a corner above this leading to a notch in the rock. Start some 50ft/15m down from the top of the gully at a ledge and flake belay. Move up the step of rock onto the slab. Descend the edge of this to make a rightward traverse across to gain the higher, smaller, slab and climb the steep corner crack above to gain The Notch. Climb straight up the arête above to a large block-flake then step right into the gully and climb a narrow slab to finally step right to a recess. Climb the gully above exiting up the rock rift onto easy ground. The top of Pillar Rock, known as High Man, lies some30ft/10m above. It is usual to abseil off the top, from a suitable rock spike near the edge (50ft/15m), into the rift of Jordan Gap. Otherwise retrace your line of ascent. From the gully a steep path leads directly up the hillside to the summit of Pillar Mountain. Follow the main path eastwards along and down the shoulder to find the top of Black Sail Pass.

LINGMELL (ENNERDALE), 1427FT/435M; STEEPLE, 2687FT/819M; SCOAT FELL, 2760FT/841M; HAYCOCK, 2617FT/797M; LITTLE GOWDER CRAG, 2405FT/733M; CAW FELL, 2288FT/697M; ENNERDALE FELL, 2113FT/644M

Maps: OS OL4, L89: GR 142130, GR 157117, GR 160114, GR 145107, GR 141110, GR 132110, GR 123119
Access point: Ennerdale youth hostel, GR 142141.
NB: vehicular access into the valley, apart from those with a pass authorised by the Forestry Commission, is prohibited. The distance from the car park beneath Bowness Knott to Char Dub Bridge is 2mls/3km
Distance/ascent: 8¾ mls/3430ft, 14km/1045m
Approx time: 6 hours

From Char Dub Bridge cross the fields into the forest. A track bears left. Follow this until another track ascends diagonally rightwards through the trees. From here easy access can be made onto the open shoulder of Lingmell. The path crests the hill, with the summit cairn just above to the right. Descend slightly to cross Low Beck, then bear left and follow the north ridge falling from Steeple. Finally, impressive rock scenery leads to the summit. A little drop, then a short, steep, ascent leads to the head of Scoat Fell.

The remarkable stone wall known as The Ennerdale Fence continues from this point all the way to Ennerdale Fell and down Crag Fell to meet Ennerdale Water. Follow it, down the grassy shoulder to Haycock. Proceed to Little Gowder Crag and gain the summit cairn of Caw Fell just north of the wall. Follow the wall to the col beneath Ennerdale Fell.

PILLAR ROCK

Continue along the southern side of the wall, which from this point westwards has been reconstructed to its former splendour. The easy rise up Ennerdale Fell leads to a gate through the wall with the summit cairn beyond. From the cairn it is possible to descend directly the Silver Cove flanks of the fell, though there is no path and care should be taken to avoid the cliffs of Iron Crag. The going comprises of thick heather and rocky boulders. Alternatively return along the fell on the Ennerdale side of the wall to join the wall descending by Silvercove Beck. Where the wall bears off left, traverse right across the beck to a path descending the nose of the ridge between Silver Cove and Great Cove. The path falls easily into the forest and down to a footbridge.

SOUTH TOP of YEWBARROW, 2058FT/628M; NORTH TOP of YEWBARROW, 2021FT/616M

Maps: OS OL6, L89: GR 173085, GR 176092
Access point: Overbeck Bridge car park GR 168068
Distance/ascent: 3³/₄ mls/1950ft, 6km/595m
Approx time: 2¹/₂ hours

A short stroll along the beck leads to the steep haul up the southern ridge. A stile leads left over the fence and wall and the path traverses towards Dropping Crag. Take the higher path leading up to a gap in the rocks to its right. A vague path leads steeply up through loose scree and boulder – not very pleasant until the angle eases and further scree leads to a notch in the crest known as Great Door. Bear left to rise north up the ridge to the flattish shoulder of the mountain.

This upland plateau is easy in nature and pleasantly grassed.

Continue to the large mound forming the summit of Yewbarrow –
its Southern Top. A further ten minutes gains the cairn of the
Northern Top before the path descends the little rocky walls of
Stirrup Crag. Steep and rocky, use of hands and bottom
supplement the feet, classifying it as an easy scramble.
Alternatively an easier way can be found down a grassy slope to
the west of the Northern Top. Turning left at Dore Head, easy
descent follows the path traversing the flanks of the mountain
above Over Beck.

MIDDLE FELL, 1908FT/582M; SEATALLEN, 2270FT/692M; GLADE HOW,
1420FT/433M; BUCKBARROW, 1388FT/423M

Maps: OS OL6, L89: GR 151072, GR 140084, GR 134064,
  GR 136061
Access Point: Parking by the road at Greendale, GR 145056
Distance/ascent: 5¹/₂ mls/2395ft, 9km/730m
Approx time: 3¹/₂ hours

Rising from the road a well-defined path leads across the grass
and bracken to the steep shoulder of Middle Fell. Bear right
to climb the shoulder keeping to its right edge. The summit is
more distant than it looks – allow an hour to reach it. Descent to
the col is straightforward and from here Haycock takes on its most
imposing aspect. A steep ascent of the flanks above leads directly
to the summit plateau of Seatallen. The extensive cairn, now partly
shaped into a shelter, and the extensive dome of rubble on which it
sits is reputed to be an ancient burial mound.

Descend easily through the tussocky grass of the south-western
shoulder. A cairn marks Cat Bells. Swing left to follow the
shoulder leading towards Buckbarrow. After the initial section of
descent the going levels. A prominent rocky hillock on the right is
graced by a very well-crafted cairn: the independent top of Glade
How. Beyond, another rocky outcrop stands higher than the
shoulder and is considered to be the summit of Buckbarrow. Just
beyond, a broad gully leads down to the right to the broader west
flank of Buckbarrow. To avoid the steep, rough ground below it is
probably best to traverse across right to Gill Beck before
descending directly to the road.

10 LANK RIGG GROUP

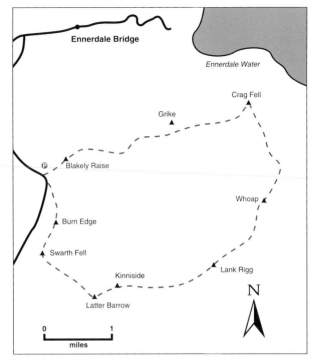

Location: South of Ennerdale on the western fringe of the Western
  Fells.
Suggested Bases: Wasdale, Nether Wasdale and Ennerdale.
Accommodation: Wasdale: self-catering and b&b at Wasdale Head,
  The Wasdale Head Inn, Wasdale Hall youth hostel; camping
  at Wasdale Head. *Nether Wasdale:* self-catering and b&b,
  The Strands and The Screes Inns; camping. *Ennerdale:* b&b;
  Ennerdale Bridge Inn, High Gillerthwaite and Black Sail
  youth hostels; no camping.

PONSONBY FELL, 1020FT/311M; STONE PIKE, 1056FT/322M; SWAINSON
KNOTT, 1118FT/341M

Maps: OS OL6, L89: GR 082071, GR 078078, GR 080084
Access point: Forestry Commission car park, Blengdale,
  GR 085053

Distance/ascent: 6¼ mls/1000ft, 10km/305m
Approx time: 2½ hours

From Wellington Bridge above Gosforth a surfaced road runs parallel to the River Bleng to reach the spacious car park – ignore any sign indicating that vehicular access is forbidden. Proceed from the car park along the road to cross the bridge. Bear left following the excellent level track through the trees and follow the east bank of the River Bleng. Where the track splits, take the high track then bear left to the wooden footbridge. Exit left to reach a surfaced road snaking up the hillside. Follow this to a junction and bear left along the forestry track. After you cross Scalderskew Beck a wooden gate on the left (signposted) leads onto the open flanks of Ponsonby Fell. After an initial boggy section the open fell is climbed without difficulty to the slightly domed grassy summit marked by a tiny cairn.

Head north across the shoulder of the fell descending to the col. Cross the the overgrown track that once connected remote Scalderskew with Calder Bridge and go through the gate then right over the stile to follow the post and wire fence through bog and rough tussocky grass. Climb up the fellside and bear left to the granite-walled enclosure of Stone Pike. Enter through one of the numerous wall gaps. Continuing north, a slight descent leads to a post and wire fence and a foot stile. There is no path, only long grass leading to the undistinguished top of Swainson Knott. This is cairnless and only a little hollow to the west indicates that peat was once extracted from the summit of this mound.

Return by the same route to the col then follow the path down past Scalderskew (beware of the dogs) and so to the wooden gate beneath Ponsonby Fell. Retrace earlier steps along the forest tracks.

BLAKELEY RAISE, 1276FT/389M; GRIKE, 1599FT/488M; CRAG FELL, 1716FT/523M; WHOAP, 1676FT/511M; LANK RIGG, 1775FT/541M; KINNISIDE, 1230FT/375M; LATTER BARROW, 1161FT/354M; SWARTH FELL (KINNISIDE), 1099FT/335M; BURN EDGE, 1050FT/320M

Maps: OS OL4, L89: GR 070135, GR 085141, GR 197144,
GR 099129, GR 092120, GR 078116, GR 074055, GR 065120,
GR 069126
Access point: Pull-off spaces beneath the flanks of Blakeley Raise beside the Coldfell Road, GR 062130
Distance/ascent: 7½ mls/2280ft, 12km/695m
Approx time: 4¼ hours

Make a direct ascent up the grassy slopes of Blakeley Raise. Follow the fence line down the shoulder to reach a sheep intake and a gate on the left leading to a short track which crosses to connect with the main forest road. Bear right here to pass a gateway in the fence beneath Grike. Swing immediately left, ascending above the track. Step over the remnants of a wire fence

THE TOP OF LANK RIGG

to continue steeply to the summit of Grike. The path descends down the shoulder left of the fence line. A stile leads over the fence crossing the heathery shoulder. At a point where the fence turns a corner, turn left. Climb to the furthest cairned outcrop of Crag Fell. Traverse south along the crest until a path down the southern nose of Crag Fell leads to a stile over the forest fence.

The descent through a break in the forest leads to a track. Turn right then take a track left which leaves the conifers over a stile beside an iron gate. Immediately in front lies the stone wall of The Ennerdale Fence. Follow the track running along the southern side of the wall to a bend below a gate in the wall. Swing right here, up onto the shoulder approaching Whoap. A path leads to the grass-domed summit. Proceed down the grassy shoulder towards Lank Rigg. At the bottom cross a dip then rise steeply to the grassy summit of Lank Rigg, marked by a stone trig point. Beyond lies a tarn and a cairned rocky bump. A little further south, follow what appears to be an ancient track striking an easy course down through the rocks to the grassy flanks below. Cross Poukes Moss in the hollow to reach the grassy bump of Kinniside before descending the shoulder to the final boulder-strewn outcrop of Latterbarrow. Descend towards the River Calder. A little lower to the right stands a small shepherd's cairn marking the easiest descent to the river. Cross to find a small section of bog which leads to higher, dryer ground and the edge of the fell bracken. It is now best to bear right until a path cuts through the narrowest portion of bracken before ascending up the open flanks of Scarth Fell to the circular summit cairn.

Descend to Burn Edge to find scattered rocks marking the actual summit on the northern end. Follow the grassy shoulder down towards the road.

11 HIGH STILE GROUP

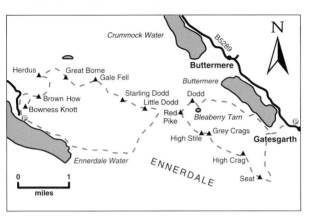

Location: Between Ennerdale and Buttermere, Western Fells.
Suggested Bases: Ennerdale and Buttermere.
Accomodation: Ennerdale: b&b; Ennerdale Bridge Inn, High
  Gillerthwaite and Black Sail youth hostels; no camping.
  Buttermere: self-catering accommodation and b&b, The Fish
  Inn, Honister Hause and Buttermere youth hostels; camping
  at Gatesgarth Farm.

BOWNESS KNOTT, 1093FT/333M; BROWN HOW (ENNERDALE),
1056FT/322M; HERDUS, 1844FT/562M; GREAT BORNE, 2019FT/616M;
GALE FELL, 1699FT/518M; STARLING DODD, 2077FT/633M; LITTLE DODD
(ENNERDALE), 1936FT/590M

Maps: OS OL4, L89: GR 112155, GR 116158, GR 118163,
  GR 124164, GR 134164, GR 142157, GR 150155
Access point: Car park beneath Bowness Knott, GR 109153
Distance/ascent: 7³/4 mls/2295ft, 12.5km/700m
Approx time: 4³/4 hours

Begin the ascent by walking back along the road from the car
park until, at the end of the woods, a stile leads onto open
brackened flanks. The path rises steeply up the hillside
bearing left slightly beneath the end of the Ennerdale Forest before
rising with the wire fence to a wooden stile. Cross this and climb
steeply up the back of Bowness Knott. Descend the same route to
the stile, cross it then rise with the wire fence until the going levels.
Bear left ascending the rocky knoll of Brown How. Descend
bearing slightly right to find a path rising up the right side of the
steep gill, Rake Beck, which descends from Herdus. As the gill cuts

---

45

into the plateau bear left rising to the summit cairn of Herdus.
From here, cross the plateau in a north-easterly fashion to
intercept the wire fence and main path which rises from Floutern
Pass. Bear right along the fence through the cleft which splits the
rocky dome of Great Borne. South of the fence stands a trig point
and ruinous summit shelter cairn – the highest top of Great Borne.
Follow the well-defined trod beside the fence. When the fence
turns sharply left leave the path. Follow the fence to the grassy
domed top of Gale Fell, marked by a stout cornerpost. Bear right
again to regain the main trod after crossing a dip. The path rises
quickly to the cairned stony top of Starling Dodd.

Across the hollow beyond, nestling a little tarn, it is only a
short way to the rock-strewn top of Little Dodd. Drop down its
bouldery face towards Ennerdale to traverse left into the top of
Gillflinter Beck. Descend by the side of the stream. As the level
eases and bracken takes hold, the path bears right away from the
stream. Follow the break between the forest to reach the
track/unsurfaced road leading back down Ennerdale.

SEAT, 1840FT/561M; HIGH CRAG (BUTTERMERE), 2442FT/744M; GREY
CRAG on HIGH STILE, 2648FT/807M; HIGH STILE, 2644FT/806M; RED PIKE
(BUTTERMERE), 2478FT/755M; DODD (BUTTERMERE), 2103FT/641M

Maps: OS OL4, L89: GR 186134, GR 180141, GR 170148,
    GR 168148, GR 161154, GR 164158
Access point: Car park by Gatesgarth Farm, Buttermere. A small
fee is payable at the farm, GR 195150
Distance/ascent: 6¾ mls/2725ft; 11km/830m
Approx time: 4½ hours

Cross the fields to the gate leading to open fell. Follow the
Scarth Gap Pass route steeply to the col. Bear right up steep
scree to find the top of Seat. Trudge up Gamlin End to the
summit cairn of High Crag. Traverse the high shoulder and ascend
towards High Stile bearing right before the summit cairn to gain
the rocky top of Grey Crag – the highest point. Cross to the
prominent cairn of High Stile then descend the shoulder before
reascending to the top of Red Pike. Take the stony path to the
saddle between Red Pike and Dodd and continue to gain the top of
Dodd. Best return to the saddle before descending the main trod to
Bleaberry Tarn. The path follows along a broken stone wall before
swinging right away from Sourmilk Gill. Follow down the zigzags
only as far as the Forest Fence then bear right along it. Continue
traversing the hillside, above the trees, on a narrow Shepherd's
path to round a craggy outcrop and find a wooden stile beyond the
end of the conifers below. Descend to the main path, which leads
to the gate beneath Scarth Gap Pass.

12 LOWESWATER FELLS

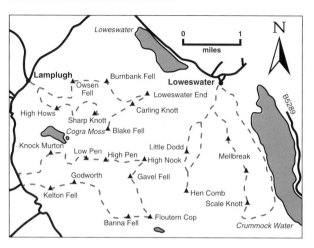

Location: Between Loweswater, Crummock Water and Ennerdale
Water, Western Fells.

Suggested Bases: Egremont, Cockermouth, Ennerdale and
Loweswater/Lorton Vale.

Accommodation: *Egremont:* limited facilities; no camping.
Cockermouth: all facilities; Double Mills youth hostel;
camping. *Ennerdale:* b&b; Ennerdale Bridge Inn, High
Gillerthwaite and Black Sail youth hostels; no camping.
Loweswater/Lorton Vale: self-catering and b&b; The Kirkstile
Inn; camping at Whinfell Hall.

KELTON FELL, 1020FT/311M; GODWORTH, 1197/365M; BANNA FELL,
1496FT456M; FLOUTERN COP, 1480FT/451M; GAVEL FELL, 1726FT/526M;
HIGH NOOK on GAVEL FELL, 1601FT/488M; HIGH PEN, 1558FT/475M; LOW
PEN, 1427FT/435M; KNOCK MURTON, 1467FT/477M

Maps: OS OL4, L89: GR 095181, GR 101183, GR 116174,
GR 122174, GR 117185, GR 120189, GR 111189, GR 105190,
GR 095191

Access point: Side of the Croasdale to Lamplugh road just above
the junction to Rowrah, GR 087183

Distance/ascent: 6¹/₂ mls/2035ft, 10.5km/620m

Approx time: 4 hours

By the signpost 'Kirkland 1, Rowrah 2' a gate opens onto a
track. Follow this until after the next gate a stile on the right
leads to the top of Kelton Fell. Continue to stride over a low

fence and on to the grassy top and small cairn of Godworth. Climb
the shoulder above then bear right descending past sheepfolds into
the upper ravine of Croasdale Beck. Cross the stream and contour
to pass Grain Gill before climbing to the left of High Bridge Gill to
gain the shoulder of Banna Fell and on to its undistinguished
grassy top. Pass the old boundary fence and descend left of a
modern wire fence before climbing up the knoll of Floutern Cap.
Descend and bear right over boggy ground to follow the fence line
rising over White Oak to the summit cairn of Gavel Fell. High
Nook is reached by following a direct but pathless course over the
rough heather.

Descend then head for Fothergill Head to take a stile over the
fence. Take the grassy track before moving right onto the shoulder,
descending this to step over the fence and gain the top of High
Pen. Descend to Low Pen and continue to the forestry track. Bear
right descending towards the dammed Cogra Moss before finding a
path rising steeply left through the trees. A stile leads onto open
fell and a steep ascent is made directly to the top of Knock
Murton. Descend the shoulder to the first iron workings then bear
left directly down to the track beneath. Follow this to a stile then
gain the line of the old railway track and follow this back to the
road.

OWSEN FELL, 1342FT/409M; BURNBANK FELL, 1558FT/475M;
LOWESWATER END on CARLING KNOTT, 1703FT/519M; CARLING KNOTT,
1785FT/544M; BLAKE FELL, 1878FT/573M; SHARP KNOTT, 1581FT/482M;
HIGH HOWS (LAMPLUGH), 1027FT/313M

Maps: OS OL4, L89: GR 101209, GR 110209, GR 121206,
GR 117203, GR 110197, GR 107201, GR 096202
Access point: Lamplugh, opposite the church, GR 089209
Distance/ascent: 6mls/1705ft, 9.5km/520m
Approx time: 3¹/₂ hours
Access problems: At the time of writing landowner/tenant Mr
Richardson of Howgill, Lamplugh objects to the use of the
track and entry onto Owsen Fell. This route is described by
A. Wainwright, *The Western Fells*, 1966.

From The Green in Lamplugh take the stile and track
(signposted footpath) leading through the fields. Beyond a
double gate a sign indictes that a footpath turns to the right.
This route, however, takes the track to the left rising up the hill to
the edge of the forestry. A stile left of the gate provides access.
Follow the track bearing left at a junction to reach the far side of
the plantation to exit over a stile. The track bears left alongside the
edge of the forestry passing through a gate. Go left over a fence to
reach open fellside. Continue by the edge of the forestry to find
remnants of an old fence line leading on to the top of Owsen Fell.
Cross to the dip beyond and up to the top of Burnbank Fell. An
old iron fence post marks the spot.

Follow the fence line first making slight descent and then take the stile over the fence line cutting across in front. Stride over the fence to the left and and contour around the head of Holme Beck towards the Loweswater End of Carling Knott, marked by cairns and a rock shelter. Descend the rocky south-eastern edge of the shoulder to a hollow then make a steep rise, crossing a wire fence near the top, to reach the summit of Blake Fell. Proceed down the shoulder to locate a path bearing off left to Sharp Knott. A short steep ascent above a col leads to the top. Return to the col and descend the grassy path steeply to the head of Wisenholme Beck as it enters the forestry. A track to the left is followed to a junction and the right fork taken. Beyond a left bend in the track a path breaks off to the right leading to a stile. Stride the low fence on the left and follow the edge of the field by the stone wall. At the highest point bear right to the grassy mound of High Hows. Descend the field in the direction of Lamplugh bearing left to a gate in the first wire fence. Soon a gate leads to a track which descends to a track traversing below. Turn right along this track to return to Lamplugh.

HEN COMB, 1670FT/509M; LITTLE DODD (LOWESWATER), 1188FT/362M

Maps: OS OL4, L89: GR 132181, GR 132192
Access point: Kirkstile Inn car park Loweswater Village, GR 142209. Landlord allows patrons' parking. Don't park and walk – ask permission first.
Distance/ascent: 4mls/1310ft, 6.5km/400m
Approx time: 2 hours

 Follow the lane leading over Church Bridge and past Kirkgate Farm. Pass ancient earthworks to enter Mosedale. Cross the beck and follow the path along the west bank beneath the flanks of Hen Comb. Prior to reaching mine workings, now grassed over, ascend diagonally up the hillside to the shoulder. Continue to ascend the domed head of Hen Comb. Retrace steps down the shoulder continuing to the little outcrop of Little Dodd. The path continues to the fell wall then bears right, back down to Mosedale Beck.

NORTH TOP of MELLBREAK, 1670FT/509M; SOUTH TOP of MELLBREAK, 1678FT/512M; SCALE KNOTT, 1109FT/338M

Maps: OS OL4, L89: GR 143195, GR 148185, GR 150178
Access point: As per previous route, GR 142209.
Distance/ascent: 5mls/1950ft, 9km/595m
Approx time: 3¾ hours

As per the previous walk pass the earthworks to find a path bearing left. Ascend the open northern shoulder of Mellbreak, rising diagonally leftwards then zigzagging through scree and

---

heather. At the top of the scree a short gully leads to open fellside.
A path continues up the nose all the way to the North Top of
Mellbreak. Continue over the saddle of heather and bilberry to
reach the higher Southern Top of Mellbreak. Descend the
southern shoulder of the mountain to make the slight rise to the
top of Scale Knott. Descend south again to meet a wire fence, cross
this and pick the easiest line to gain a well-defined track above the
Black Beck, this is Floutern Pass. Follow this passing the
confluence with Scale Beck bearing left to the shore of Crummock
Water. Follow the path heading north along the lakeside. A stile
and a gate pass Highpark after which the road continues to Park
Bridge. Beyond take the left fork back to Loweswater Village.

13 FELLBARROW GROUP

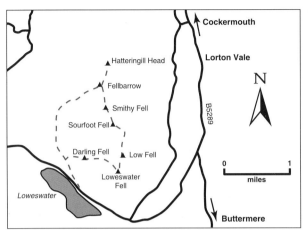

Location: North of Loweswater, the most northerly of the
  Western Fells.
Suggested Bases: Cockermouth and Loweswater/Lorton Vale.
Accommodation: *Cockermouth:* all facilities; Double Mills youth
  hostel; camping. *Loweswater/Lorton Vale:* self-catering and
  b&b; The Kirkstile Inn; camping at Whinfell Hall.

DARLING FELL, 1283FT/391M; LOWESWATER FELL, 1352FT/412M; LOW
FELL, 1388FT/423M; SOURFOOT FELL, 1348FT/411M; SMITHY FELL,
1286FT/392M; FELLBARROW on MOSSER FELL, 1363FT/416M;
HATTERINGILL HEAD on WHIN FELL, 1263FT/385M

Maps: OS OL4, L89: GR 128225, GR 136223, GR 137226,
  GR 135233, GR 133237, GR 132242, GR 133248
Access point: Car park above the western end of the lake,
  GR 122224
Distance/ascent: 6mls/1805ft, 9.5km/550m
Approx time: 4 hours

Take the road above the lake to find a surfaced track signed
'Mosser Unfit For Cars.' Follow this until a sign on the
'Public Footpath Foulsyke.' Go over the stile and ascend the
steep path crossing the stile to the top of Darling Fell. Descend into
the hollow of Crabtree Beck and cross it by the fence. Climb for a
short way before bearing right to the rocky knoll of Loweswater
Fell. Follow the good path up the nose to the cairned top of Low
Fell. Cross the dip and go over the stile beyond to follow a grass

LOOKING DOWN TO THE FELLBARROW GROUP FROM GRASMOOR

track then over another stile bearing left to the top of Sourfoot
Fell. Descend to the short section of stone wall and rise to the top
of Smithy Fell. Continue over a stile and ascend the flanks of
Fellbarrow to find a stone trig point on the summit. Follow the
fence down the dip beyond and take the stile over the stone wall.
Skirt the scree then ascend Hatteringill Head of Whin Fell, the
most northerly top of the Western Fells. Return to the summit of
Fellbarrow and descend westwards down the slopes of Mosser Fell.
Cross the Moss to a short track over Mosser Beck and through a
gate onto the track/road. Turn left and head back.

14 DALE HEAD GROUP

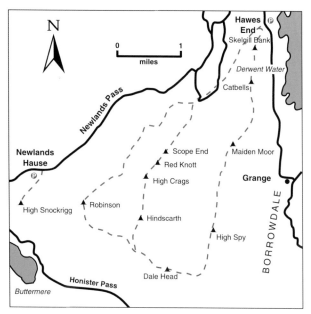

Location: Between Borrowdale, Buttermere and Newlands, North Western Fells.

Suggested Bases: Keswick, Borrowdale, Buttermere and Newlands.

Accommodation: Keswick: all facilities except railway station; Longthwaite youth hostel; camping at The Headlands (Derwent Water), Castlerigg Hall and Castlerigg Farm. *Borrowdale:* Barrow House youth hostel; b&b at The Scafell Inn; camping at Ashness Farm, Dalt Wood-Grange, Stonethwaite, Thornythwaite and Seathwaite farms. Bus service from Keswick. *Buttermere:* self-catering accommodation and b&b, The Fish Inn, Honister Hause and Buttermere youth hostels; camping at Gatesgarth Farm. *Newlands:* self-catering and b&b; The Swinside Inn; camping at Braithwaite Village.

SKELGILL BANK, 1109FT/338M; CATBELLS, 1481FT/451M; MAIDEN MOOR, 1890FT/576M; HIGH SPY on SCAWDEL FELL, 2143FT/653M; DALE HEAD, 2472FT/753M; HINDSCARTH, 2385FT/727M; HIGH CRAGS (NEWLANDS), 1736FT/529M; RED KNOTT, 1483FT/452M; SCOPE END, 1352FT/412M

Maps: OS OL4, L90: GR 245206, GR 244198, GR 237182,
    GR 234162, GR 223153, GR 216165, GR 217175, GR 221180,
    GR 224183
Access point: Car park at Hawes End, GR 248212
Distance/ascent: 10mls/2855ft, 16km/870m
Approx time: 5¹/₂ hours

A well-worn path climbs from the road to the blunt nose of
Skelgill Bank. An easy shoulder continues to a steeper climb
up the bell-shaped dome of Catbells. Easy walking leads to the
rise up Maiden Moor before the path splits. Keep to the right along
the flat edge of the moor above Newlands Valley. A small cairn on a
rise denotes the top of Maiden Moor. Easy walking continues with
the path climbing gently to the northern end of the High Spy
shoulder of Scawdel Fell. Continue along the flat shoulder to the
cairn marking High Spy, the top of Scawdel Fell – sometimes
known as Lobstone Band. Easy descent leads across the stream
above the head of Newlands and rises to traverse by Dalehead
Tarn. Climb steeply to the top of Dale Head. Descend Hindscarth
Edge, two rocky knolls lead to a third lower but distinctly separate
pinnacle (unnamed), marked by a substantial and ancient cairn.
Continue until an easy ascent leads up the Buttermere end of
Hindscarth. Follow the crest of the shoulder to the summit cairn.
Follow the broad back of Hindscarth to a large, ancient circular
shelter, after which the edge steepens dramatically. Take care until
the little top of High Crags brings an easing in the angle. The main
path passes beneath the top of Red Knott and leads to Scope End.

From Scope End the path steepens to a wire fence. Bear right
above Low Snab Farm (which serves teas during the summer
months). Cross the footbridge over Newlands beck and proceed
along the track to Little Town. A lane on the right, signposted
Skelgill', leads to a house and then continues across open fields. It is
easy to follow and leads to the surfaced road beyond Skelgill Farm.

SCOPE END, 1352FT/412M; RED KNOTT, 1483FT/452M; HIGH CRAGS (NEW-
LANDS), 1736FT/529M; HINDSCARTH, 2385FT/727M; ROBINSON, 2418FT/737M

Maps: OS OL4, L90: GR 224183, GR 221180, GR 217175,
    GR 216165, GR 202169
Access point: Small car park above Chapel Bridge, Little Town,
    Newlands Valley, GR 232194
Distance/ascent: 6¹/₂ mls/2495ft, 10.5km/760m
Approx time: 4 hours

Follow the road to cross Newlands Beck via Chapel Bridge
then bear left to Newlands Church. Turn left down the track
leading to Low Snab Farm and pass through the farmyard to a
gate. The path bears right to the snout of the ridge then steeply
climbs Scope End above Goldscope Mine. Next comes Red Knott and
High Crags before a steep ascent leads to the shelter cairn on the edge
of Hindscarth. The path leads easily to the summit. Continue along

ON HINDSCARTH LOOKING OVER TO HIGH SPY

the shoulder to a path junction. Bear right to climb the Littledale Edge. A gentle ascent leads above Robinson Crag and past Hackney Holes. As the angle eases you reach the summit plateau before bearing right to the summit cairn of Robinson.

Descending from the summit a cairn marks a distinct steepening in the ridge. As Blea Crags are reached the route changes direction slightly, bearing left and descending over three rocky steps. The path is well-defined and the technical difficulties slight, though the position is dramatic. Easier going follows the sharp edge of High Snab Bank. The path bears right, making a straightforward grassy descent to a track and gate. Follow the track past Low High Snab after which the road leads past Newlands Church.

HIGH SNOCKRIGG, 1726FT/526M

Maps: OS OL4, L90: GR 187169
Access point: Car park at the summit of Newlands Pass (Newlands Hause), GR 193176
Distance/ascent: 1¹/₄ mls/655ft, 2km/200m
Approx time: 1 hour

A well-worn path leads directly to the Moss Force (often referred to as Newlands Hause Waterfall). Continue steeply up to the right of the fall, following a natural weakness. For a short way the going is steep and exposed and involves a little easy scrambling. The climb quickly crests the gentle edge of Buttermere Moss to follow the raised grassy rim of the plateau. Continue easily to the summit cairn of High Snockrigg. Return along the edge of the moss. The path bears left before reaching the point taken in ascent from the waterfall. With one or two steeper steps it winds down to Newlands Hause.

15 GRASMOOR GROUP

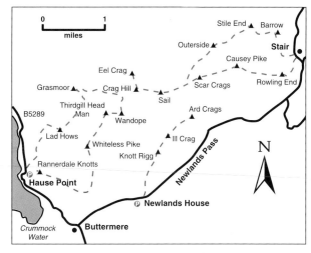

Location: North of Newlands Pass, between Buttermere and
  Borrowdale, North Western Fells.
Suggested Bases: Keswick, Borrowdale, Buttermere and
  Newlands.
Accommodation: Keswick: all facilities except railway station;
  Longthwaite youth hostel; camping at The Headlands
  (Derwent Water), Castlerigg Hall and Castlerigg Farm.
  Borrowdale: Barrow House youth hostel; b&b at The Scafell
  Inn; camping at Ashness Farm, Dalt Wood-Grange,
  Stonethwaite, Thornythwaite and Seathwaite farms. Bus
  service from Keswick. *Buttermere:* self-catering
  accommodation and b&b, The Fish Inn, Honister Hause and
  Buttermere youth hostels; camping at Gatesgarth Farm.
  Newlands: self-catering and b&b; The Swinside Inn; camping
  at Braithwaite Village.

ROWLING END, 1421FT/433M; CAUSEY PIKE, 2090FT/637M; SCAR CRAGS,
2205FT/672M; SAIL, 2536FT/773M; CRAG HILL, 2751FT/839M; EEL CRAG,
2649FT/807M; OUTERSIDE, 1863FT/568M; STILE END, 1467FT/447M;
BARROW, 1494FT/455M

Maps: OS OL4, L90: GR 229207, GR 219209, GR 207206,
  GR 198203, GR 193204, GR 190207, GR 211215, GR 221219,
  GR 227218
Access point: Stoneycroft, parking along the verge either side of
  bridge, GR 232212

SNOW-CAPPED CRAG HILL, LEFT OF CENTRE WITH CAUSEY PIKE TO THE RIGHT OF CENTRE

Distance/ascent: 6³/₄ mls/3280ft, 11km/1000m
Approx time: 4¹/₂ hours

From the stone-arched bridge across Stoneycroft Gill climb directly up the grassed hillside. Numerous old tracks and water leats are crossed before the path bears left to the heathery shoulder of Rowling End. Easy progess along the shoulder crosses Sleat Hause to the nose of Causey Pike. The edge rears impressively and the climb is steep. Near the top hands as well as feet may be needed. Beyond the rocky summit dome the hill forms a cockscomb crest, with alternate peaks and troughs, before dropping to the shoulder. Rise to the top of Scar Crags. Beyond the summit cairns the going steepens in descent to the col of Sail Pass. A long diagonal ascent leads up the flanks of Sail with a little detour right to reach the summit cairn.

Returning to the path the going takes on the atmosphere of an alpine ridge with cliffs plunging away on both sides. A little pinnacle leads to steeper ground as the edge climbs towards the summit dome of Crag Hill. A cairn marks an ease in the angle from where the final approach to the trig point lies over a stony gently-domed plateau. Reached by descending slightly to the north, the separate top of Eel Crag is marked by an ancient cairn. Follow the same route in return to Sail Pass. Turn left descending steeply at first then more easily. Before reaching High Moss the path meets a track, leave it in a short way to bear left across High Moss before climbing the nose of Outerside to its summit cairn.

A straightforward descent and ascent lead to the top of Stile End. Bear right and descend to the grassy hollow of Barrow Door. An ascent leads to the heather clad summit of Barrow. Direct descent down the southern flank of Barrow involves a short steep section of thick heather before the easier open shoulder of fell grass is reached. There is no distinct path yet it is the quickest way back to Stoneycroft. From the shoulder make a simple descent to the mine track above Stoneycroft Gill and follow this until a path bears off down to the right.

KNOTT RIGG, 1824FT/556M; ILL CRAG (NEWLANDS), 1791FT/546M; ARD CRAGS, 1906FT/581M

Maps: OS OL4, L90: GR 197189, GR 200192, GR 207198
Access point: Car park at the summit of Newlands Pass –
  Newlands Hause, GR 193176
Distance/ascent: 3¹/₂ mls/1230ft, 5.5km/375m
Approx time: 2 hours

Climb to the nose from where the path becomes straightforward. Take easy grassy slopes past a number of rocky outcrops of Skiddaw Slate. Beyond a final bump the angle leans back and a grassy stroll leads to the highest grassy knoll, the top of Knott Rigg. The middle bump of the shoulder, Ill Crag, arrives quickly. Beyond the dip in the ridge and its tiny tarn, the shoulder gathers momentum. It rises distinctly to its highest top, the heather clad dome of Ard Crags. Return by the same route.

LAD HOWS, 1398FT/426M; GRASMOOR, 2795FT/852M; WANDHOPE, 2533FT/772M; THIRDGILL HEAD MAN, 2402FT/732M; WHITELESS PIKE, 2165FT/660M; RANNERDALE KNOTTS, 1165FT/355M

Maps: OS OL4, L90: GR 172193, GR 175203, GR 188197,
  GR 184196, GR 180190, GR 167182
Access point: Parking area by the roadside where the track leaves
  for High Rannerdale, beneath Rannerdale Knotts, GR 163184
Distance/ascent: 6¹/₄ mls/2950ft, 10km/900m
Approx time: 4 hours

The track beneath Rannerdale Knotts leads through a gate and bears right to a footbridge over Squat Beck. Bear left along the track and take the gate/stile past the stone wall. Just beyond to the right, a path begins to lead directly up the hillside. After an initial section of ascent it bears left to strike a diagonal line through the bracken, emerging onto a grassy shoulder above Cinderdale Beck. After a short section of ascent it bears right to find the grassy summit bump and cairn of Lad Hows. The ridge beyond, although rising through heather and Skiddaw slate above, is quite straightforward and leads to a cairn marking the edge of Grasmoor's summit plateau. Proceed to the large shelter cairn which marks the highest point. There are numerous ancient cairns along the summit plateau, marking the points where the main paths arrive and descend. Strike a course, well-defined, to the easternmost cairn perched on an elevated top. The path falls

GRASMOOR RISING ABOVE LORTON VALE

directly to the col between Grasmoor and Crag Hill. At this high-level crossroads the way lies straight on up the steep flanks of Crag Hill. Bear right to intercept the steep edge above Addacomb Hole. Follow the edge to the cairn of Wandhope.

A simple descent leads to the cairn (man) of Thirdgill Head Man. From the col a short steep ascent leads to the rocky summit of Whiteless Pike. The path descends steeply towards Whiteless Breast and bears right, slightly slackening in gradient, before finally steepening again to drop to the col above High Rannerdale. Climb slightly then follow the crest of Low Bank. Pass over a cairned rocky top to a second, higher, cairned rocky top. This is the summit of Rannerdale Knotts. The path continues north a little (take care: steep crags lie beyond) before bearing left to descend the nose of Rannerdale Knotts, making directly for Hause Point. A saddle is reached and a short, steep, finish down to the right leads to the start.

16 GRISEDALE PIKE GROUP

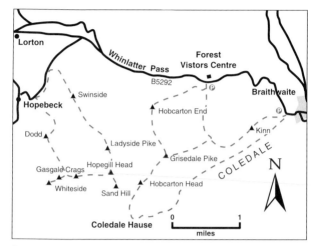

Location: South of Whinlatter Pass, between Lorton Vale and
Coledale, North Western Fells.
Suggested Bases: Keswick, Braithwaite, Cockermouth,
Buttermere, Loweswater/Lorton Vale.
Accommodation: *Keswick:* all facilities except railway station;
Longthwaite youth hostel; camping at The Headlands (Derwent
Water), Castlerigg Hall and Castlerigg Farm. *Braithwaite:*
limited facilities including inns and campsite. *Cockermouth:*
all facilities; Double Mills youth hostel; camping. *Buttermere:*
self-catering accommodation and b&b; The Fish Inn, Honister
Hause and Buttermere youth hostels; camping at Gatesgarth
Farm. *Loweswater/Lorton Vale:* self-catering and b&b;
The Kirkstile Inn; camping at Whinfell Hall.

HOBCARTON END, 2080FT/634M; GRISEDALE PIKE, 2593FT/791M

Maps: OS OL4, L90: GR 194220, GR 199226
Access point: Car park in Hospital Plantation forest opposite and
below the Visitors' Centre above Grisedale Gill, Whinlatter
Pass, GR 209242
Distance/ascent: 3³⁄₄ mls/1705ft, 6km/520m
Approx time: 2¹⁄₂ hours

Take the track beneath the car park crossing the stream and
rising to a junction. Bear right for a short way until an
overgrown track rises to the left. The path rises onto open fell
to leave the forest and climb the heathery slopes above Black Crag.
Along the north ridge of Grisedale Pike the path reaches the first

GRISEDALE PIKE: LAKELAND'S MATTTERHORN

of three cairns on Hobcarton End. The other two cairns lie beyond a post and wire fence which is crossed via a stile. The middle cairn, although the least substantial, stands at the highest point. From the col the ascent gradually steepens. You then join the line of the ruined wall which ascends the north-east ridge to the summit of Grisedale Pike. Head east from the summit down the east ridge. This is not obvious from above and a compass bearing may be necessary in bad weather. The path soon becomes well-defined, though is steep throughout. The ridge eases to a rounded shoulder over Sleet How. The route bears left until stopped by the forestry fence of the Hospital Plantation. Drop down to the left beside the fence where a vague path descends through thick heather. In the bottom of Grisedale Valley bear left. Cross the gill to find a gate leading through the fence and onto a forest track. Bear right, cross a little bridge and follow the track directly back to the car park.

KINN, 1227FT/374M; GRISEDALE PIKE, 2593FT/791M; HOBCARTON HEAD, 2425FT/739M

Maps: OS OL4, L90: GR 219233, GR 199266, GR 194220
Access point: Limited parking in old quarry alongside the B5292
    Whinlatter Pass road above Braithwaite Village, GR 227237
Distance/ascent: 6¹/₂ mls/2085ft, 10.5km/635m
Approx time: 3¹/₂ hours

A path climbs the flanks of the hill to the right of the parking area. It offers a gentler approach than the more direct route which climbs from the elbow in the bend of the road below. Once the shoulder is gained it gives a straightforward ascent over the gentle top of Kinn. Pass the natural spring of Lanty Well to the

left. Steeper ground leads to the shoulder of Sleet How. The final
section of the east ridge steepens to the pyramidal head of
Grisedale Pike. Pass the summit cairn and descend the south-west
shoulder. Cross a small rise over the bump of Hobcarton Head
(unnamed on the OS). Before the path levels, follow another path
down to the left. It leads diagonally down the hillside to Coledale
Hause. Below lies the upper basin of Coledale with High Force
waterfall plunging into it. From the crossroads of Coldedale Hause
follow the distinct path which takes the southern edge of the basin.
This picks up a mine track and leads safely past Force Crag to
cross Coledale Beck below the mine buildings. Make an easy
return down Coledale via the mine track.

DODD (LORTON), 1489FT/454M; EAST TOP of WHITESIDE, 2359FT/719M;
WEST TOP of WHITESIDE, 2319FT/707M; GASGALE CRAGS, 2306FT/703M;
HOPEGILL HEAD, 2525FT/770M; SAND HILL, 2480FT/756M; LADYSIDE
PIKE, 2306FT/703M; SWINSIDE, 1670FT/509M

Maps: OS OL4, L90: GR 169231, GR 175221, GR 171220,
  GR 173222, GR 186222, GR 187219, GR 185227, GR 177239
Access point: Above the gate on the little road behind Hopebeck,
  GR 169242
Distance/ascent: 6mls/2655ft, 9.5km/810m
Approx time: 3¹/₂ hours

From the road the path skirts the stone wall before dropping
to cross Hope Beck by the stone sheepfold. Climb to intercept
an ancient grassed track and follow it, rising to the left. The
path steepens after passing a ruined building. Shortly after this
bear right, up steep heathery slopes to the summit cairn of Dodd.
A ridge extends to the col behind. Descend it to the left to find a
vague path rising up the ridge above. The path cuts through rough
heather. The going is never steep and finally leads to the East Top
of Whiteside. This is the highest point, though the top to the west
takes a higher profile from the valley. Return to the main top and
proceed along the knife-edge ridge. Cross the flat table top of
Gasgale Crags. Descend into a hollow and then climb to Hopegill
Head. The stroll to Sand Hill is simple. A steep descent leads north
down the rocky head of Hopegill Head. The path falls due north
from the summit. It is initially extremely exposed, with the
precipice of Hobcarton Crag to the right. The exposure diminishes
as the path moves away from the edge, to descend a stepped rocky
slab. When the angle eases, traverse a rocky knoll on the left to
gain the line of an old wall. This leads to Ladyside Pike. Continue
down the shoulder to the field boundary junction where the angle
eases. Walk along the left side of the wall and continue down the
shoulder. The wall becomes a fence and the highest point of
Swinside lies just to the right. The ancient cairn that once
represented the top of Swinside lies lower and further to the right.
To reach this stride the fence. Most will be content to follow the
fence directly down to the road just above High Swinside Farm.

17 LORD'S SEAT GROUP

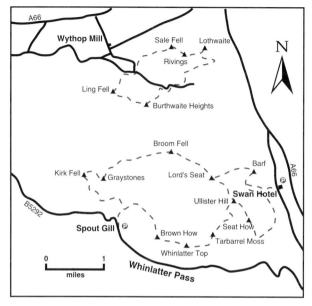

Location: North of Whinlatter Pass between Lorton Vale and
    Bassenthwaite Lake, North-Western Fells.
Suggested Bases: Braithwaite, Cockermouth, Lorton Village.
Accommodation: Braithwaite: limited facilities including
    inns and campsite. *Cockermouth:* all facilities; Double Mills
    youth hostel; camping. Lorton: limited facilities including inns;
    camping at Whinfell Hall.

BARF, 1536FT/468M; LORD'S SEAT, 1811FT/552M; ULLISTER HILL,
1722FT/525M; SEAT HOW (THORNTHWAITE), 1627FT/496M

Maps: OS OL4, L90: GR 215268, GR 204266, GR 209260,
    GR 213256
Access point: Directly beneath Barf there is pull-in space by the
    side of the old A66 opposite the Swan Hotel, GR 220264
Distance/ascent: 4mls/1870ft, 6.5km/570m
Approx time: 2¼ hours

Follow the road for a few yards. A kissing gate on the right
leads to the foot of the scree beneath the face of Barf. Above
stands the unmistakable figure of The Bishop of Barf

(regularly whitewashed, he is known locally as The White Bishop). The path bears left and crosses Beckstones Gill. Climb a stile over a wire fence. The path then rises steeply and as larch turns to conifer, a craggy outcrop is encountered. The path follows a natural fault. It leads right at first then back left to make a technically easy ascent through the barrier. Above, the path rises steeply to emerge onto a forestry track (Junction No. 21). Bear right to find a path which leads to a stile over the boundary fence of the forest. After crossing the head of Beckstone Gill the path winds around the face of Barf. It then emerges onto the little rocky perch which constitutes the top.

The well-defined path descends into the hollow beyond the summit. It then re-ascends to the shoulder which falls from Lord's Seat. As the angle steepens the final pull to the grassy dome of Lord's Seat begins. After a short distance the top is gained. A swift descent of Lord's Seat's south flank leads to a stile over the boundary fence of Thornthwaite Forest. The Forestry Commission have constructed a splendid path over the bogs and through the heather. Where the path splits (Junction No. 5), take the left fork. After a few yards, a vague path strikes off right climbing through heather to the summit of Ullister Hill. Descending southwards and now skirting the edge of the conifers, a corridor through the trees opens to the left. Follow this; the path descends quickly down the nose of Seat How to meet a broad forestry track. Take this through the pines to a junction (No. 9) and bear left. The track levels and at a Junction No.8, bear right. Descend beneath rock cuttings. This track is the one intercepted by the original footpath which rises beside Beckstones Gill.

BROWN HOW on WHINLATTER, 1696FT/517M; WHINLATTER TOP, 1722FT/525M; TARBARREL MOSS, 1617FT/493M; ULLISTER HILL, 1722FT/525M; LORD'S SEAT, 1811FT/552M; BROOM FELL, 1676FT/511M; GRAYSTONES, 1496FT/456M; KIRK FELL on LORTON, 1437FT/438M

Maps: OS OL4, L90: GR 191251, GR 197249, GR 206253, GR 209260, GR 204266, GR 194272, GR 178264, GR 173266
Access point: Spout Gill Car Park, GR 181256
Distance/ascent: 6³/₄ mls/2065ft, 11km/630m
Approx time: 4 hours

The track leads to the lane of Darling How. Bear right and follow the lane past the farm. Pass through two gates before a third in a stone wall leads to a break in the conifer plantation. Although thickly covered with Corsican pine the trees stand in parallel lines which allow relatively easy access. Climb through the pine trees to reach a fence. Bear left along it to find a stile which leads onto a forestry track. Immediately above, an avenue sweeps through the trees to emerge, through a gap in the fence, onto open hillside. The gap is closed by a section of timber-framed fence that can be opened for entry. Ascend the open hillside directly to the top of Brown How. The summit is marked by a semi-circular stone shelter with an open view to Hobcarton Crags and Grisedale Pike.

A grassy path leads along to the small cairned summit of Whinlatter Top.

Descend down the shoulder to the boundary fence of Thornthwaite Forest. Climb to the little cairned top of Tarbarrel Moss and a corner in the fence. A stile leads to a little path falling to the main forestry track. Cross this and bear right along a track. When this splits, bear left until another path breaks off to the right. This skirts the forest to gain a little hollow then rises to the summit of Ullister Hill. A path falls quickly down the heathery shoulder to meet an excellent path. After an extensive boggy area, which is crossed dry by the path, climb to the open grassy shoulder of Lord's Seat. A stile leads to the summit. A straightforward ridge gives access to Broom Fell. Its summit cairn stands immediately west of the ruinous stone wall which traverses the summit from north to south. The highest point lies slightly south-east of the cairn. Walk down the shoulder to cross through a gap in the stone wall. Follow the edge of Darling How Plantation over Widow Hause. At the end of the plantation a gate gives access to a grassy track which leads diagonally up the hillside to the left. Follow this track, first left then right, to an open shoulder. Walk to the left to a cairned grassy bump. This is the north top of Graystones. The true summit lies on a little rocky knoll a little further to the south.

From the latter continue past an obvious circular pit and rise with the stone wall to a rocky head and junction of stone walls. A stony descent leads to the little col to the west. A gentle rise continues to the summit of Kirk Fell. The summit is marked by a cairn of small stones and a wooden post. Descend steep grassy slopes to enter Sware Gill by an old stone wall. Cross the gill and follow a ruined stone wall across the fellside to the edge of Darling How Plantation. Descend directly along its edge until a stile gives access to a forest track. Follow this until a cleared break drops steeply right to the banks of Aiken Beck just above Spout Force. Follow a path on the right until the beck can be crossed. A little section of ascent leads to a fenced-off viewing point for Spout Force. Climb the break above the viewing point to regain the track which leads back to the car park.

LING FELL, 1224FT/373M; BURTHWAITE HEIGHTS, 1043FT/318M; LOTHWAITE, 1132FT/345M; RIVINGS, 1099FT/335M; SALE FELL, 1178FT/359M

Maps: OS OL4, L90: GR 180286, GR 189283, GR 203297, GR 198294, GR 194297

Access point: An old quarry provides parking space beside the road (leading to Kelswick Farm) above Brumston Bridge in the Wythop Valley, GR 185293

Distance/ascent: 4¼ mls/1560ft, 7km/475m

Approx time: 2¼ hours

 Follow the road across Brumston Bridge and climb the steep hill which bears right, opposite the buildings of Eskin. The road levels and is joined by two tracks. Take the gate on the

BARF RISING FROM THE VALE OF BASSENTHWAITE

right. Join the old Copse Road across the open hillside, passing a track which merges from the left. A short distance beyond this a vague path leads up through the bracken. It follows the edge of a tiny stream which is fed by a small spring that issues from a pile of stones. Above the spring the path continues up a hollow past a pile of stones to a terrace. Ascending this, pass numerous piles of stones until it is better to bear left and climb more directly. Pass another terrace which bears a track rising from the right. Walk over a series of natural terraces to the top of Ling Fell. There is a stone trig point and a cairn a little further to the east. Head straight down the heathery flanks in the direction of Burthwaite Heights to a field with a curved and stepped edge. A vague path steers south across the moss to the bank of a drainage ditch. Follow this to an iron gate. Beyond the gate follow the right bank of another ditch then continue up the flank of Burthwaite Heights. The gently sloping grassy table top is highest at its northern edge.

Descend to the east. Join the line of a stone wall and follow it to an iron gate just above the plantation. Descend to a grassed track and bear right along it. The path ends with a gate leading onto the surfaced road which runs up the Whythop Valley. Pass Old Scales Farm and continue up the road to a sign 'Public Bridleway' on the left (the second, there is also one opposite the farm). Follow this (signed) across the fields to Chapel Wood. Bear right along the leafy and muddy track. When you leave the wood pass a gate. Bear left, then left again when the track splits. Shortly afterwards a smaller track, rising diagonally left, cuts a well-defined course through the whin bushes. Before reaching a grassy shoulder bear right. Make a more direct ascent of the hillside to reach a long grassy shoulder. Bear right along this to a rocky outcrop which marks the summit of Lothwaite. Head back along the shoulder until at, a pile of stones, bear left up the grassy

ON LORD'S SEAT LOOKING OVER TO SALE FELL AND LOTHWAITE

hillside to the unmarked top of Rivings. Follow a grassy track through two ruined stone walls. This leads to a ridge and small cairn, which marks the summit of Sale Fell. The path descends centrally down the shoulder, with the flat plain of the west coast of Cumbria in front. A natural grassy corridor leads between rocky piles of quartz before decending to a stone wall. Bear left and make a steep descent back to the road and gate just above the old quarry.

18 BLENCATHRA GROUP

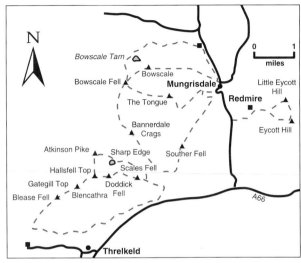

Location: North of Threlkeld, Northern Fells.

Suggested Bases: Threlkeld and Mungrisdale.

Accommodation: Threlkeld: self-catering and b&b; Horse and Farrier and White Horse inns; camping at Burns Farm and Setmabanning; bus service from Keswick to Penrith. *Mungrisdale:* self-catering and b&b; Old Crown Inn and Carrock Fell youth hostel at Heskett Newmarket; camping barn; no campsite.

Maps: OS OL5, P576, L90: GR 387295, GR 385301

Access point: Opposite a stile and signpost 'Public Footpath', GR 368295, by the side of the Mungrisdale road. Limited parking

Distance/ascent: 3mls/490ft, 5km/150m

Approx time: 1³/₄ hours

Climb the stile over the fence and cross the field following the fence line to a further stile/gate. Continue by the wall to Barrow Beck and a stone slab bridge. Cross the bridge and bear left along the riverbank to a gate in a stone wall. Continue along the bank to the track just below the ruinous barn of Westing. Cross the track, by the end of a bridge. Continue to a small gate which gives

access to a field. Walk through the field by the bank of Barrow
Beck, crossing a narrow side stream by a ruined stone-slab bridge.
At the top of the field the wall is ruined and there is open access to
the fellside. Cross Naddles Beck, and strike a line up the hillside
through some boggy going then long grass and rushes. Rise to the
spine of a long rock ridge. Cross the boggy canyon behind and
continue up to a level plateau beneath some craggy outcrops. Walk
directly up the steeper ground above to the summit of Eycott Hill.
Strike a line due north, passing a little walled bield (in ruins) before
descending into the dip and crossing the stream. Above stand three
little tops. The middle one, fringed with small crags, is Little Eycott
Hill. Descend the hillside, avoiding the rocky bluffs, until it can be
traversed to pick up the line of ascent and crossing of Naddles Beck.

BOWSCALE FELL, 2305FT/702M; THE TONGUE, 1814FT/553M

Maps: OS P576, OL5, L90: GR 333304, GR 344302
Access point: Bowscale, limited parking by the roadside,
  GR 358317
Distance/ascent: 5¾ mls/1525ft, 9km/465m
Approx time: 3 hours

Where the road enters the village and narrows to make a tight
turn through the buildings, a path turns off to the left. Beyond
the gate, the grassed path rises easily to the tarn. Above to the
right, a grassy rake cuts through the steep rocky basin to exit onto
the shoulder above Tarn Crags. An easy ascent leads first to a
cairn then to a ruined stone shelter, which marks the top of
Bowscale Fell. A gentle slope descends before rising again to the
highest point of The Tongue. A path leads down to the right, along
the edge of its craggy eastern face. The path joins a track by an old
stone bield. Bear left along the track. Cross Bullfell Beck where it
joins the River Glenderamackin, to pass houses and join the road
by a telephone kiosk in Mungrisdale. Follow the road, past the
church, back to Bowscale.

EAST TOP on BOWSCALE FELL, 2185FT/666M; BOWSCALE FELL, 2305FT/702M; BANNERDALE CRAGS, 2240FT/683M; SOUTHER FELL, 1713FT/522M

Maps: OS P576, OL5, L90: GR 340310, GR 333304, GR 335290,
  GR 355292
Access point: Mungrisdale, verge parking near the road junction,
  GR 364306
Distance/ascent: 6¾ mls/2395ft, 11km/370m
Approx time: 3¾ hours

Above the road junction take the gated track to the left of the
quarry – now housing a Water Authority building. Just past
the quarry, a small path rises to the right, directly up the

THE RIDGES OF BLENCATHRA VIEWED FROM THE SOUTH

hillside. Initially the path is vague, though the route through the gorse and bracken is quite clear. Above this, hill grass predominates. A small rise (cairned) leads to the higher cairned East Top of Bowscale Fell. Descend to the dip. Rise again, passing first a cairn then a ruined stone shelter which marks the summit of Bowscale Fell. Aim south and descend the broad grassy shoulder until it begins to level. At this point bear left to pick up a well-defined sheep trod which traverses the rim of Bannerdale Crags. A broad slab of rock sweeps up from a steep, dark gully before the path ascends to a gravestone-shaped cairn. The summit actually lies a little way to the west and is marked by a pile of large flat slates. Drop down the grassy shoulder over the steeper lower slopes, known as White Horse Bent. Cross a grassed track leading to the wooden footbridge over the young River Glenderamackin. Rise up the track to Mousthwaite Col then bear left. A vague path up the grassed fellside forming the southern shoulder of Souther Fell leads to a substantial circular cairn. Strike a line over the level top of the fell to a single rock on a tiny outcrop. This is the highest point of Souther Fell. Continue, losing height gradually, to the northern edge of the summit plateau, then steeply down the nose. Beyond a stone wall and little field, a gate opens onto the road opposite The Mill Inn in Mungrisdale. Unfortunately a sign on the wall (once taken by a stile) says 'Keep Out', so make a detour along the wall to the left until it turns in the direction of the winding River Glenderamackin. Cross the river by the most convenient boulders (only possible in dry conditions) to gain the track which leads into Mungrisdale by the telephone kiosk.

BLENCATHRA

SCALES FELL, 2238FT/682M; DODDICK FELL TOP, 2434FT/742M;
HALLSFELL TOP on BLENCATHRA, 2847FT/868M; GATEGILL FELL TOP,
2792FT/851M; BLEASE FELL, 2638FT/804M

Maps: OS OL5, L90: GR 332279, GR 329277, GR 323277,
GR 318274, GR 312270
Access point: Lay-by along the A66 above Threlkeld, GR 339267
Distance/ascent: 6mls/2295ft, 9.5km/700m
Approx time: 3¹/₂ hours

Pass the road-side cottage and bear left rising to open fellside.
A path, cut deep through the grass and bracken, rises
diagonally across the hillside to the right. Climbing the craggy
edge above Mousthwaite Comb, the path splits. Go left up the
grassy shoulder of Scales Fell. The second and higher bump
constitutes the summit of this, Blencathra's most easterly fell. Skirt
the rim of the upper bowl feeding Scaley Beck and ascend to the
rocky head of Doddick Fell. Continue up the shoulder to Hallsfell
Top, the summit of Blencathra. The south-westerly traverse along
the edge of the south face includes the distinct rise of Gategill Fell
Top. The most westerly top reached is Blease Fell. The going, over
small shingly Skiddaw slates or close-cropped turf, proves to be
flat and easy. A straightforward descent, down the grassy shoulder
leads to a distinct track. This cuts a course diagonally east down
the hillside. The path is followed to a stone wall before descending
directly down to the fell wall. Bear left along the waymarked path,
which traverses the hillside above the fell wall. In turn, cross Gate
Gill, Doddick Gill and Scaley Beck before finding the opening back
to the A66.

ATKINSON PIKE (FOULE CRAG), 2772FT/845M; HALLSFELL TOP on
BLENCATHRA, 2847FT/868M

Maps: OS OL5, L90: GR 325283, GR 323277
Access point: The lane leading off from the A66 by the White
    Horse Inn leads to a car park, GR 349272
Distance/ascent: 5mls/2625ft; 8km/800m
Approx time: 2 hours

This route involves a litle rocky scrambling and considerable
exposure. The path ascends into Mousthwaite Comb and out
onto the col above. Bear left and follow the path traversing
the hillside above the Glendermackin River to join Scales Beck.
Climb to Scales Tarn then bear right. A stony climb leads to the
ridge of Sharp Edge. Traversing the crest needs a cool head. The
most difficult section crosses a polished slab which becomes
dangerously slippery when wet or verglassed. Below to the north
lies an easier path beneath the crest. Towards the end of the ridge
the ground steepens and it is best to follow a chimney groove just
right of the edge. Finally the angle falls back and Atkinson Pike is
reached. Easy going into the trough and up to Hallsfell Top follows
the actual saddle of 'Saddleback' – the alternative name for
Blencathra. From the summit cairn descend directly down Hall's
Fell Ridge, steep and exposed for the first 250m. The rocky path is
well-defined though caution should be exercised. The going eases
as descent is made to the fell wall. Bear left and follow the path
along the wall which eventually leads back to the car park.

19 SKIDDAW MASSIF

Location: North of Keswick, Northern Fells.
Suggested Bases: Keswick, Skiddaw House and Bassenthwaite.
Accommodation: Keswick: all facilities except railway station;
   Longthwaite youth hostel; camping at The Headlands
   (Derwent Water), Castlerigg Hall and Castlerigg Farm.
   Skiddaw House: youth hostel. *Bassenthwaite:* limited
   facilities;self-catering and b&b; The Sun Inn; no youth hostel;
   camping at Traffords.

SALE HOW, 2185FT/666M; SOUTH TOP of SKIDDAW, 3034FT/925M;
MIDDLE TOP of SKIDDAW, 3044FT/928M; HIGH MAN on SKIDDAW,
3053FT/931M; NORTH TOP of SKIDDAW, 3024FT/922M; HARE CRAG,
1765FT/538M

Maps: OS P576, OL4, L90: GR 276286, GR261285, GR 261288,
   GR 260291, GR 261292, GR 277299
Access point: Latrigg car park, GR 281254. Alternatively Skiddaw
   House youth hostel, GR 287291.
Distance/ascent: 11mls/2130ft, 18km/650m
Approx time: 4¹/₂ hours

Turn left from the head of the car park, following the main tourist route up Skiddaw. Immediately after turning left onto the shoulder a grassed track bears off to the right. Follow it to enter the great fault corridor of Glenderaterra Beck and continue through to find a gate/stile into the Calder Valley and the area known as Skiddaw Forest. Ahead of the path a larch plantation can be seen with a few ruined buildings beneath. After crossing a wooden footbridge over Salehow Beck, Skiddaw House becomes visible on the edge of the larches. To the right of the plantation a grassy path leads up to Sale How. Beyond the highest point is a little bump with a cairn. From the col beyond continue up the flanks of Skiddaw to intercept the main tourist path. Bear right to cross a wire fence. The path leads to the stony summit ridge of Skiddaw. It then traverses South Top and Middle Top before reaching the large shelter and trig point of High Man – the summit of Skiddaw.

Proceed north passing the little cairn which marks the North Top and drop to the north col. (Alternatively, missing out Hare Hill, you can return to the car park by descending the tourist route directly to Latrigg car park). Bear right, making an easy descent down the shoulder of Blake Hill to the little top of Hare Hill. A swathe through the thick heather extends across Dead Beck directly to the road leading to Skiddaw House.

LATRIGG, 1207FT/368M; LONSCALE PIKE, 2306FT/703M; LONSCALE FELL, 2344FT/715M; JENKIN HILL, 2411FT/735M; LESSER MAN on SKIDDAW, 2674FT/815M; LITTLE MAN on SKIDDAW, 2837FT/865M; SOUTH TOP of SKIDDAW, 3034FT/925M; MIDDLE TOP of SKIDDAW, 3044FT/928M; HIGH MAN on SKIDDAW, 3053FT/931M; CARL SIDE, 2447FT/746M

Maps: OS OL4, L90: GR 279247, GR 289273, GR 286271, GR 274275, GR 269276, GR 267278, GR 261285, GR 261288, GR 260291, GR 255281

Access point: Keswick, by the end of Spooney Green Lane, behind Briar Rigg housing estate, GR 268241

Distance/ascent: 10mls/3675ft, 16km/1120m

Approx time: 5½ hours

Proceed up Spooney Green Lane (signposted 'Public Bridleway Skiddaw'), taking the bridge over the A66 and past a gate by a house. Continue up the hill through a further gate until a lane branches off to the right. At this point, marked by two stone gateposts, a path climbs directly up the hillside skirting the edge of the larch wood. The highest little rocky knoll reached marks the summit of Latrigg. Continue along the dyke, traversing the rim of the hill. On reaching a stone wall bear left. At the end of the wall a stile leads down to a track on the right which is followed to the head of the car park. Turn right and follow the avenue between the wall on the left and the wire fence on the right, to meet a kissing gate and the open shoulder. Bear right on the track,

crossing Whit Beck, to the stile/gate running down the edge of
Lonscale Fell. Climb left along the fence to follow the edge of
Lonscale Crags directly to the little upturned point of Lonscale
Pike. Walk across the shoulder to the summit cairn of Lonscale
Fell. Continue to a ruined wall and fence. Take the gate on the
right and continue along the fence. Rise again until the going slackens. A cairn, marking the flat top of
Jenkin Hill, stands over the fence to the right. It is necessary to
stride the fence to reach it but just beyond there is an old iron gate
taken by the main tourist track. After crossing the line of the fence
bear left. Climb steeply, first to Lesser Man then up to the final
rocky top of Low Man.

Descend to the col with the fence line to your right. Ascend
directly to join the main tourist route at the end of the main ridge
of Skiddaw. South Top and Middle Top lead in turn to High Man,
its shelter and trig point marking the summit of Skiddaw. Return
to the cairn of Middle Man then bear right to find a path which
makes a diagonal descent over the screes of the western flank. At
the col by Carlside Tarn bear left. Ascend to the broad summit and
cairn of Carl Side. The rough stony path descends to White
Stones. Cross an old wall and the craggy Doups before a stile
leaves the brackened hillside. Field grass leads to a little lane
beside a house. Bear left along the surfaced road through
Applethwaite, rising to turn right at the junction by the hotel. Now
descend the road past Birkett Wood Farm until, on the left a sign
points 'Public Footpath' through a kissing gate. Follow the path
through the fields to round the house beside Spooney Green Lane.
Re-join the original track back to the start.

DODD (SKIDDAW), 1647FT/502M

Maps: OS OL4, L90: GR 244274
Access point: Dodd Wood car park, by The Old Sawmill tea room,
    GR 235281
Distance/ascent: 3mls/1610ft, 5km/490m
Approx time: 2 hours

Above the building of The Old Sawmill and to the right of Skill
Beck a series of steps lead up through the forest. Climb these
and the path beyond, to gain a forest track. Continue up this
to a junction and bear right. In 25 metres a path cuts off through
the forest on the left beside a green marker post. This climbs
steeply at first through dark conifer until the path levels and
swings right to traverse the face of the hillside. Rising again the
path intercepts another forestry road. Continue in the same
direction across the junction, to join a forestry track which
ascends to the right. This steepens and begins to zigzag until at a
col on the southern shoulder of Dodd a sign reads 'Dodd Summit
300m'. Follow the steepening path to the left. Enter the summit
mop of trees by a steep rocky knoll. After first levelling the path
rises again to the summit cairn of Dodd. Take the same path back

to the col and turn left along the track. This passes beneath the craggy shoulder of Long Doors. The path falls to a larger forest road. Descend this, bear right at the junction. Continue down the track bearing left at a further junction to keep Skill Beck on the left. A little way further a marker post indicates a path which breaks off to the left. This contours back to a wooden footbridge over the beck. The path continues to a forestry track. Descend this to find the original junction in 200 metres. Find the steps back to The Old Sawmill.

WATCHES, 1093FT/333M; ULLOCK PIKE, 2270FT/692M; LONG SIDE, 2408FT/734M; CARL SIDE, 2447FT/746M; MIDDLE TOP of SKIDDAW, 3044FT/928M; HIGH MAN on SKIDDAW, 3053FT/931M; NORTH TOP of SKIDDAW, 3024FT/922M; BROAD END, 2726FT/831M; BAKESTALL, 2208FT/673M; COCKUP, 1657FT/505M

Maps: OS P576, OL4, L90: GR 241304, GR 244288, GR 249284, GR 255281, GR 261288, GR 260291, GR 261292, GR 261298, GR 266307, GR 259314

Access point: Lay-by at the side of the Orthwaite road beyond the A591 junction above Bassenthwaite Village, GR 237311

Distance/ascent: 6¾ mls/3330ft, 11km/1015m

Approx time: 4 hours

Just above the lay-by a sign reads 'Public Bridleway'. Take the stile and follow the track leftwards over the stream until a zigzag can be made to the right. The grassed track, initially lined by ancient thorns on the uphill side, leads across the field and rises to a stile/gate after which bear right off the track. Ascend the field by the wall to a narrow gate through the fell wall. This leads onto the toe of the edge. Ascend this directly to the distinctive summit of Watches. Numerous bumps are ascended before the going steepens to the shapely cone of Ullock Pike. A twin higher bump further on proves to be the significantly higher top of Ullock Pike. Longside Edge ascends to the rocky top of the ridge known as Long Side. After a short descent the path rises up the grassy flanks of Carl Side. At the high point, strike rightwards across the summit plateau to find the cairned top of Carl Side. Follow a well-defined path down to the col and tarn. A diagonal path then rises to the left across the great scree flanks. This emerges on the summit shoulder of Skiddaw by the cairn/shelter of Middle Man. Continue north along the summit ridge to High Man – the highest top of Skiddaw. Descend north to find the little cairn of the North Top, then a col, before rising to the plateau of Broad End. Despite numerous little cairns the actual top is illusive. Bear right and follow the line of the wire fence down the shoulder to the cairned top of Bakestall. The way lies to the left.

Descend the grassy flanks. Cross Dead Beck above the trees and the old mine entrance. Then head out onto the summit of Cockup. Near the edge of Cockup Gill find an ancient track which leads to a gate through the fell wall. The path leads down through

SKIDDAW MASSIF

the field following the line of the wall. Cross through a gate and follow a track. Just before the road, bear left following another track. This passes Mill Beck and rises to a field with an old pit to the right. A gate on the left gives access to a vague path which contours the field. This eventually joins a track which descends to a wooden bridge over Barkbeth Gill below Hole House. Climb towards the building but then bear left following the sign 'Public Bridleway'. In a short distance a sign 'Permissive Path' will be found and should be followed (ignore the sign 'Public Bridleway'). It leads to Barkbeth Farm and then directly onto the footpath which runs along the wall above. This emerges through a gate into a field passing a well-worn rubbing stone. It then contours left to a little gate which leads onto the original track.

20 NORTH O'SKIDDAW GROUP

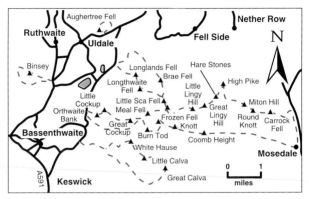

Location: North of Blencathra and Skiddaw, Northern Fells.

Suggested Bases: Mungrisdale, Bassenthwaite, Uldale, Caldbeck and Heskett Newmarket.

Accommodation: *Mungrisdale:* self-catering and b&b; camping barn; no campsite. *Bassenthwaite:* limited facilites; self-catering and b&b; The Sun Inn; camping at Traffords. *Uldale:* limited facilities; b&b. *Caldbeck:* limited facilities; self-catering and b&b. *Heskett Newmarket:* limited facilities; self-catering and b&b; The Old Crown Inn; Carrock Fell youth hostel.

CARROCK FELL, 2174FT/663M; ROUND KNOTT, 1978FT/603M; MITON HILL, 1991FT/607M; HIGH PIKE (CALDBECK), 2157FT/658M; HARE STONES, 2057FT/627M; GREAT LINGY HILL, 2021FT/616M; LITTLE LINGY HILL, 1998FT/609M; KNOTT, 2329FT/710M; COOMB HEIGHT, 2057FT/627M

Maps: OS P576, L90: GR 342336, GR 334337, GR 329341, GR 319350, GR 315344, GR 310340, GR 304339, GR 296330, GR 311327

Access point: Above the Mosedale to Caldbeck road, past Stone Ends Farm. A short track leads to numerous parking places, GR 353338

Distance/ascent: 10½ mls/2510ft, 17km/765m

Approx time: 5½ hours

Rake Trod rises diagonally leftwards on the hillside, beneath the crag. Follow this into a gill, by two Scots pines, then rise directly up the heather-clad shoulder above. Pass a cairn to ascend a steep knoll of heather and boulders. The path leads on to cross the stone wall of the summit hill fort. Rise to the summit cairn of Carrock Fell, which is situated on a high rock plinth above the western edge of the wall. Cross the wall and descend the shoulder, bearing left to go around the bog. Climb up to a circular bandstand of rock with a flat grassy top. This is Round Knott. Proceed past a cairn and scattered rock outcrops, to the flat table top of Miton Hill.

Descend into the dip beyond, Red Gate, to find an intersection of tracks. Ascend the shoulder by way of a track until a path branches off right, skirting the top of Dry Gill and then rising up the shoulder of High Pike. The top of High Pike is marked by a large pile of rocks, a stone bench and a trig point. A path leads south back down the shoulder past an old collapsed mine entrance. Briefly join the substantial miners track that has risen across the eastern flanks of High Pike and at its highest point bear right to find the few stones on Hare Hill. Descend over heather into the dip to a wooden plank conveniently crossing a water-filled peat hag. Climb to Great Lingy Hill, which is marked by a small cairn. Beyond lies the dome, with a cairn which must be Little Lingy Hill (the OS accredit an insignificant bump across Miller Moss with this name). A short way beyond, a little stream cutting drops into the ravine of Roughton Gill. Directly opposite, above an old mine entrance which looks unstable, a groove/channel cut into the hillside leads up Balliway Rigg. Climb through rough, boggy ground to reach the grassy shoulder which rises to Knott, the centre pin and highest of these fells, which puts the whole of this sprawling group into perspective. Head east down the shoulder to cross the boggy plateau of Rigg and on to the cairn and defined top of Coomb Height. The path descends along the crest of the shoulder. As it begins to steepen a long ditch is crossed. Danger -- do not follow it. This is the top of a collapsed mineral outcrop, where the ore has been extracted to a considerable depth underground. Continue down the shoulder to the track. Cross the bridge and follow the road by the delightful waters of the River Caldew. Pass the 'Friends Meeting House 1702' and bear left into the hamlet of Mosedale.

GREAT CALVA, 2265FT/690M; LITTLE CALVA, 2106FT/642M; WHITE HAUSE, 1525FT/465M

Maps: OS P576, L90: GR 291312, GR 282315, GR 272324
Access point: Lay-by beside the Orthwaite road, GR 249324.
Distance/ascent: 6³/₄ mls/1705ft, 11km/520m
Approx time: 3¹/₄ hours
Access Problems: Mr R.Mawdlsey of Dash Farm has made general objection to walking on 'areas of Skiddaw' – this route lies entirely above the fell wall save where it passes through a gate onto a track leading to the publicly adopted road; much of the route was detailed by A.Wainwright in *The Northern Fells*, 1962.

 Take the 'Public Bridleway' signposted opposite Peter House Farm up the surfaced road through a gate and continue through the fields via three more gates. Where the road falls to

Dash Beck the bridleway, signed 'Skiddaw House', bears off up to the right. Follow it through a gate/kissing gate and under Dead Crags. The track rises above Whitewater Dash falls, and crosses a gate/stile below Birkett Edge. It then crosses a small bridge and rises again. Continue along the track until it begins to fall. It crosses Dead Beck and turns towards Skiddaw House. Bear left and climb the flanks of Great Calva. As height is gained the vague path swings right to climb the heathery nose of the pyramid. A boulder field adorns what appears to be the summit with a small shelter before the cairn, but this southern tip of Great Calva is not actually the highest point. The ridge rises to rocks and a fine cairn marking the summit. It is best to follow the line of the ruined fence to avoid the bog on the route to Little Calva. The cairn and highest point lie just south of the fence line. Proceed down the shoulder to pick up a track which leads rightwards to White Hause. Leave the track, climbing right, to a boulder of volcanic origin, which defines the top. Walk down the steep flanks to cross the track and continue to Dash Farm. A gate opens directly onto a track which leads through the farm to become the original surfaced road.

ORTHWAITE BANK, 1142FT/348M; LITTLE COCKUP, 1296FT/395M; GREAT COCKUP, 1726FT/526M; MEAL FELL, 1804FT/550M; LITTLE SCA FELL, 2083FT/635M; GREAT SCA FELL, 2135FT/651M; KNOTT, 2329FT/710M; FROZEN FELL, 2050FT/625M; BURN TOD, 1952FT/595M

Maps: OS P576, L90: GR 256335, GR 262337, GR 273333, GR 283337, GR 290342, GR 291339, GR 296330, GR 287332, GR 283329

Access point: A Public Bridleway leaves the road just south of Orthwaite, a wide verge allows limited parking -- do not block any field entrances or the road, GR 253337

Distance/ascent: 7¹/₂ mls/2115ft, 12km/645m

Approx time: 3³/₄ hours

Follow the bridleway through the gate, then ascend left by the wall. Carry on in the same line climbing the open fellside. Continue past an interestingly shaped boulder to the summit of Orthwaite Bank. Little Cockup is the prominent hill to the left. Traverse left to the boulder which marks its top. Afterwards work back right to the nose of Great Cockup to a level plateau and cairn below the final tower. Ascend leftwards, crossing a diagonal line of shooting butts. Walk to the prominent cairned western tip of Great Cockup. According to the OS the highest point is a slight grassy rise in the middle of the plateau to the east. A small cairn marks the top of Great Cockup. Cross the summit plateau over another rise. Follow the path track down by a little slate edge into Trusmadoor. Cross the gap and take the track which rises across the southern flank of Meal Fell. After a little way bear left. Ascend directly to the summit outcrop of rock, which is marked by a large circular shelter.

Descend east to the col. Find a prominent grassy rake which

leads diagonally left up to the gap between Great Sea Fell and Little Sea Fell. Go left to the cairn and shelter on Little Sea Fell. A straightforward path leads to the broad top of Great Sea Fell and on to the summit plateau of Knott. Make a rough descent to the grassy shoulder of Frozen Fell. Contour south over feeder streams, peat hags and long grass onto the declining shoulder of Burn Tod. The shoulder rises slightly to a single white quartz rock marking the top of Burn Tod. Beyond lies a short stone wall. Immediately down to the right lies a distinct path/track. This zigzags down the hillside, to Trusmadoor. Cross the stream and bear left along the path above Burntod Gill. When the path diverges take the lower, more distinct path, to the stone bield. Follow the path across the basin of field grass and rise up again following the bridleway. The track falls gently to eventually join a level track. Bear right at the junction and continue to the road.

LONGLANDS FELL, 1585FT/483M; LOWTHWAITE FELL, 1670FT/509M; LITTLE SCA FELL, 2083FT/635M; BRAE FELL, 1923FT/586M

Maps: OS P576, L90: GR 276354, GR 278347, GR 290342, GR 289352
Access point: Longlands. Parking space by the water pumping station below the hamlet, GR 266358
Distance/ascent: 4^1/$_2$ mls/1675ft, 7.5km/510m
Approx time: 2 hours

Pass through the gate just above the pumping station and immediately bear right. Break off left and ascend the grassy shoulder. Keep to the edge on the right of some hollows to reach Thwaite. Continue directly above to the cairned top of Longlands Fell. A grassy track runs over the top, having risen from the north and descends into the dip in the shoulder beyond. Follow it and rise to the top of Lowthwaite Fell. Descend to Broad Moss and cross it to re-discover the grassy track. Follow it to eventually bear left beneath the summit of Little Sca Fell. Ascend to the cairned top and pit shelter of Little Sca Fell. Cross the plateau to find a track which descends the shoulder towards Brae Fell. The going is easy and rapid progress is made before ascent leads to the bouldery cap of Brae Fell. Fall down the grassy shoulder bearing slightly left to find another vague grassy track. This leads down to the ford at Charleton Wath. Bear left to follow the track to Longlands.

BINSEY, 1466FT/447M

Maps: OS P576, L90: GR 225355
Access point: On the road towards Bewaldeth there is an iron gate and a wide verge parking area, GR 235352
Distance/ascent: 2^1/$_2$ mls/575ft, 4km/175m
Approx time: 1^1/$_4$ hours

BINSEY

Enter the sheep pen by the gate and exit this by another on the left. Bear left beneath the grassed hollow of a long-deserted quarry and find a vague grassy trod that leads directly to the summit. The pyramidal top of Binsey is found to be a long ridge of dark rock. The large pile of boulders is recognised as an ancient tumulus and there are numerous shelters. A cairn stands at the highest point and the trig point just beyond it. Continue in the same direction to another long whaleback ridge of rock. It is cairned and offers an open vista. Descend with the craggy shoulder of West Crag rising to the left. Beneath this, bear left. There are a number of paths at different levels that contour the hillside. Continue traversing above the stone wall until the path drops through the clusters of ancient hawthorn.

GREEN HOW on AUGHERTREE FELL, 1053FT/321M

Maps: OS P576, L90: GR 258375
Access point: Large car park over the brow of the hill above
　　Uldale, GR 262374
Distance/ascent: 1¹/₂ mls/165ft, 2.5km/50m
Approx time: ¹/₂ hour

The most northerly fell within the Lake District National Park. To make a walk take an anticlockwise circular tour. Cross to the old limestone quarry, which is usually flooded. Bear right over the rough fell grass to the little cone of Dale Hows. On the northerly flanks, below ancient earthworks, lie circular ditches and mounds. Pass them and walk over to a stone wall. Elfa Well lies along the wall. From here make the short climb to Green How. The car park lies below.

21 GREAT MELL GROUP

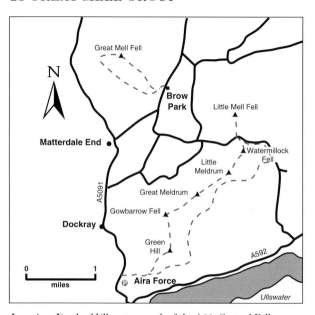

Location: North of Ullswater, south of the A66, Central Fells.

Suggested Bases: Matterdale, Ullswater and Penrith.

Accommodation: Matterdale: limited self-catering and b&b; Royal
Hotel in Dockray; camping at Rookin House Farm.
Ullswater: self-catering and b&b; Brotherswater and
Traveller's Rest inns; Patterdale and Helvellyn youth hostels;
Swirral camping barn above Glenridding; camping at Sykeside
by Brotherswater, Side Farm in Patterdale, various sites
above Watermillock and east of the lake are to be found Park
Foot, Hill Crest and Waterside House; bus service from
Penrith to Patterdale and Penrith to Keswick. *Penrith:* all
facilities except youth hostel and camping.

GREAT MELL FELL, 1762FT/537M

Maps: OS OL5, L90: GR 397254

Access point: An unsurfaced lane leaves the Matterdale End to
Motherby road beneath the south-eastern toe of the fell,
GR 406247

Distance/ascent: 2³/₄ mls/920ft, 4.5km/280m

Approx time: 1¹/₂ hours

Walk along the rough unsurfaced lane, past a gate and stile on the right to a second gate and stile. Stride this and follow the path, bearing left above the fell wall/fence. After leaving the mixed decidious woods, a vague grassy path rises to the right. This makes a circuitous climb to the shoulder of the fell. Continue up the shoulder passing through the western extremity of an apparently ancient planting of Scots Pine. The shoulder levels and thick, tussocky grass leads to the top. Continue in the same direction, towards Troutbeck. Make a steep descent to an old fence line above the disused rifle range. The path extends in two directions around Great Mell Fell. Either bear right, to make a clockwise traverse through woods, back to the first gate mentioned, or go left and make an open anticlockwise route back around the foot of the fell to the initial point of ascent. An alternative start can be made from the bend in the A5091 (GR 390266), just outside the hamlet of Troutbeck, where a path leads alongside the old rifle range. Once the open fell is gained the hill can be ascended or descended at virtually any point.

GREEN HILL on GOWBARROW PARK, 1450FT/442M; GOWBARROW FELL, 1579FT/481M; GREAT MELDRUM, 1434FT/437M; LITTLE MELDRUM, 1325FT/404M; WATERMILLOCK FELL, 1391FT/424M; LITTLE MELL FELL, 1657FT/505M

Maps: OS OL5, L90: GR 408214, GR 408218, GR 415223, GR 425233, GR 423240
Access point: National Trust car parks: Park Brow above A5091 (free) and below Aira Force waterfall (toll), GR 398206
Distance/ascent: 8mls/2200ft, 13km/670m
Approx time: 4¼ hours

Descend through the wood below the Park Brow car park on the constructed path which leads to a gate and an open field beyond. Enter the wood surrounding Aira Force by another gate. Take the high path left across the stone-arched bridge perched above the brink of the main fall. Bear left then right to a stile leading to open fellside. Ascend directly along a path to top the rocky knolls of Hind Crag and Bernard Pike. Climb to reach the fine cairn marking the top of Green Hill. The best path along the top initially keeps to the left. It picks a course through the humps of heather, bilberry and the lows of cotton grass before topping a higher grassy bump. It finally falls beneath a rocky knoll. Go round this to see a higher craggy knoll – the summit of Gowbarrow Fell topped by a trig point. Take the path eastwards down the steep snout of a crag. Follow it until a vague path bears left. Climb a stile where the stone wall makes a corner. Contour right to meet the edge of the wire fence bounding the Swinburn's Park forestry plantation. Rise with it then continue directly up the grassy hillside to the highest point of Great Meldrum. Continue east across a saddle, formed from red de-natured rock. Walk easily down the grassy shoulder to a distinct corner in the fence

LOOKING OVER TO GREAT MELL FELL

line. Climb the fence and bear right to skirt the edge of the conifers. Pass the head of a track which breaks through the trees. Fall and rise through thick grass past bushes of gorse, to the furthest and highest rock outcrop. This is the summit of Little Meldrum. (Alternatively follow the track then bear left to reach the same point).

A pond lies in front. Descend to the left of this to pick up a track. Follow this through the trees to a gate in the wall. Continue along the track then bear right to ascend the slopes of Watermillock Fell. The top of the fell is cleaved by a canyon which runs south to north. Descend to the track and follow it to the gate onto the road. Bear right, past the fenced reservoir compound to take the second gate on the left. This is signposted conflictingly 'Public Footpath' and 'No Public Right Of Way To Top Of Fell' with a 'Bull In Field' sign thrown in for good measure! Climb through the field to a stile/gate which leads to the open flanks of Little Mell Fell. A grassy runnel leads directly up the steep fellside to a banked path traversing the hillside. Cross this to reach the trig point that marks the top of Little Mell Fell. Return to the road. Descend to find a sign which marks the return to Aira Force through a gate on the right. Traverse beneath the craggy flanks of Watermillock Fell to rise to the shoulder above Hagg Wood. Traverse above Swinburn's Park, now a forestry plantation, to exit via a stile over the fence. Cross the stream and take a second stile over a wall. Bear left past the ruins of an old shooting lodge. Cross a gill and wooden bridge to round a rocky knoll in spectacular fashion. Continue to where the path splits. Take the lower branch which leads around the spur of Green Hill onto its face above Ullswater. Continue along the path descending behind Lyulph's Tower. Take the track rising to the right which leads back to the stone-arched bridge above Aira Force.

22 DODDS GROUP

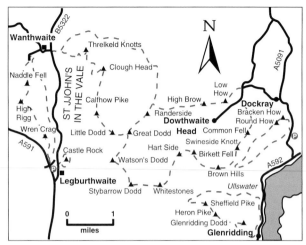

Location: South of Threlkeld, east of St John's In The
Vale/Thirlmere and west of Matterdale/Ullswater, the head of
the Central Fells.

Suggested Bases: Matterdale, Thirlmere, Threlkeld and Ullswater.

Accommodation: Matterdale: limited self-catering and b&b; Royal
Hotel in Dockray; camping at Rookin House Farm.
Thirlmere: Youth hostel; b&b at the King's Head Inn;
camping at Bridge End Farm and Dale Bottom. Bus service
from Ambleside to Keswick. *Threlkeld:* self-catering and b&b;
Horse and Farrier and White Horse inns; camping at Burns
Farm and Setmabanning; bus service from Keswick to
Penrith. *Ullswater:* self-catering and b&b; Brotherswater and
Traveller's Rest inns; Patterdale and Helvellyn youth hostels;
Swirral camping barn above Glenridding; camping at Sykeside
by Brotherswater, Side Farm in Patterdale, various sites
above Watermillock and east of the lake are to be found Park
Foot, Hill Crest and Waterside House; bus service from
Penrith to Patterdale and Penrith to Keswick.

WREN CRAG, 1020FT/311M; HIGH RIGG, 1125FT/343M; NADDLE FELL,
1171FT/357M

Maps: OS OL5, L90; GR 316202, GR 307215, GR 309220
Access point: Car park at Legburthwaite, head of St John's in the
Vale, GR 318195
Distance/ascent: 5mls/1115ft, 8km/340m
Approx time: 2³/₄ hours

Pass through a small gate at the head of the car park onto the old road. Turn left to the kissing gate which opens onto the verge of the A591. Turn right along this over Smaithwaite Bridge. Climb over the stile and take the path which rises to the left. This leads through magnificent Scots pine. Descend steeply into the dip and take the gap in the wall. Climb again to follow along the rocky outcrops of Long Edge. A grassy incline leads to a stile over the wire fence to the left. Cross this, go right, first rising then falling to pass a little tarn in a hollow. The path descends to the left, dipping to reach a stile over a stone wall. Beyond the stile, the path runs along the wall. It then climbs to pass through a corridor formed by the rocky knoll of Moss Crag. Immediately beyond the crag turn left beneath it where there's a small tarn to the right. Make a steep ascent to the top of High Rigg. A high grassy ridge leads above the tarns of Paper Moss to a hollow and pond. Ascend to the summit of Naddle Fell (unnamed on OS map).

A wide path falls down the hillside, steepening near its end, to the buildings by the road above St John's Church. Turn right down the road past the church to a gate and stile leading to a grassy track. Skirt the foot of the fell along this track. Deviate to the right on a path taking the high side of Low Bridge End Farm. Where the track meets the bank of St John's Beck, beneath Wren Crag, the track ends and a path continues above the river, rising through the trees, to the grassy shoulder above the stile leading onto the A591.

CASTLE ROCK, 1112FT/339M

Maps: OS OL5, L90: GR 322197
Access point: Car park at Legburthwaite, head of St John's in the Vale, GR 318195
Distance/ascent: ½ ml/605ft, 0.8km/185m
Approx time: 1 hour

Leave the car park by an overgrown narrow path opposite the toilets and cross the road. Climb the steps, through the kissing gate and bear right to a gate in a stone wall. Don't take the gate but bear left by the wall to cross a track. The path rises above the track to reach the top corner of the wood. Here an aqueduct traverses the hillside and enters a tunnel. Don't take the wooden footbridge – take the stone slab stile over the wall to the right. There is a little rock face immediately above. The path follows along above the tunnel and rises to a high point amongst Scots pine. Cross the fence on the left using some stones. The path bears up through the bracken, past a rocky knoll on the left, towards the South Crag. Ascent can be made by the side of the South Crag. But the steep scree is badly eroded so it is best to make a zigzag ascent up the knoll to the right. Near the top of the knoll a gap will be found in a stone wall from where another ruined stone wall is followed. Cross a further ruined wall to gain the highest grassy break leading across Castle Rock. Before reaching the wall on the top break, move right up a rocky shoulder. Climb easily to the top of a rocky knoll. Beyond, connected by a grassy saddle is a higher stepped table of rock. Move around its right side for an easy ascent to the highest point of Castle Rock.

Descend to the saddle, bear left down to a ruined wall which runs behind Castle Rock. Bear left along it until, where it meets the crag, a gap will be found. Take this and descend to a level shoulder. A path cuts back beneath the crag. Follow this to the gully that falls between the wall of the summit tower and the North Crag. Go down a broad grassy break beneath to the base of the gully where the path descends to a gap in a stone wall. Go through and descend by the wall through the trees to find a wooden footbridge over the aqueduct. Continue down through the bracken and left onto a track to the point crossed in ascent.

THRELKELD KNOTTS, 1686FT/514M; CLOUGH HEAD, 2381FT/726M; CALFHOW PIKE, 2175FT/663M; LITTLE DODD (ST JOHN'S COMMON), 2575FT/785M; GREAT DODD, 2811FT/857M; RANDERSIDE, 2391FT/729M

Maps: OS OL5, L90: GR 330230, GR 334226, GR 331221, GR 337204, GR 342206, GR 349211

Access point: Limited parking at wide junction signposted 'Matterdale Unsuitable For Motors' above the St John's in the Vale road at Wanthwaite, GR 316231

Distance/ascent: 8mls/3000ft, 13km/915m

Approx time: 4¹/₂ hours

Take the 'Old Coach Road' lane, pass the house on the right and go through the gate to bear left at the junction. At the end of the stone wall, cross the stile over the wire fence to the right. Continues up through the old quarry tips, bearing right to a track. A signed path climbs directly up the grassy bank above the track by the side of a wire fence. Cross the stile over a wire fence and climb to cross the stile over the fell wall onto the grassy slopes of Wanthwaite Bank, at first following what appears to be a ditch/runnel in the hillside. This develops into a well-defined grassy track zigzagging up the fell. Cross through a rock cutting, passing a sheep fold below to the right. Here the track levels slightly and bends to the right. At this point bear left following a grassy path to a col. To the left there's a cairn and viewpoint, to the right the grassy summit cone of Threlkeld Knotts.

Descend, over derelict mining activity and cross the hollow. Rise over a grassy hummock to pick up the main path. The path rises first to the left then it climbs diagonally rightwards out to the shoulder. A cairn marks the head of this path. An easy ascent leads to the top of Clough Head. A broad well-defined path leads easily down the grassy flanks of Great Dodd and up to the distinct rocky knoll of Calfhow Pike. The path continues up the grassy flanks of Little Dodd to the summit cairn. Great Dodd is also reached easily and marked with a cairn.

A straightforward path leads down the shoulder from the top

to the cloven hoof stony outcrop of Randerside. To the right a
cairn marks the highest point. Follow the main path in descent to
where ponds of water lie in the peat moss. Bear left here to the
western end of Wolf Crag. There is no distinct path and the going
is a little boggy underfoot. When Mosedale Beck appears, directly
below, you are correctly located on a grassy shoulder which
descends by the western end of the crag. Circumnavigate the small
rock bluffs and descend to the Old Coach Road. Bear left and
return to Wanthwaite.

LOW HOW, 1631FT/497M; HIGH BROW, 1886FT/575M; RANDERSIDE,
2391FT/729M; GREAT DODD, 2811FT/857M; WATSON'S DODD,
2588FT/789M; STYBARROW DODD, 2766FT/843M; WHITE STONES on
GREEN SIDE, 2608FT/795M; HART SIDE, 2481FT/756M; BIRKETT FELL,
2378FT/725M; BROWN HILLS, 1808FT/551M; SWINESIDE KNOTT,
1814FT/553M; COMMON FELL, 1811FT/552M

Maps: OS OL5, L90: GR 375215, GR 368214, GR 349211,
   GR 342206, GR 336196, GR 343189, GR 353187, GR 359198,
   GR 365198, GR 378194, GR 379197, GR 383204
Access point: Parking area by the New Road/Dockray/
   Dowthwaitehead road junction at the Matterdale End of the
   Old Coach Road, GR 380218
Distance/ascent: 9mls/2525ft, 14.5km/770m
Approx time: 5 hours

Enter the grassy wastes of Matterdale Common at the eastern
end of the Old Coach Road. Immediately bear left off the
track to rise up the grassy shoulder to Low How. Descend into
the dip and rise by the stone wall, passing an ancient collapsed

WATSON'S DODD

mine level. Continue to the broad grassy summit of High Brow. Descend slightly and cross the moss beyond. Begin to rise by a small stream and continue to the main path leading up to the summit cairn of Randerside. The path steepens to the cairn and summit of Great Dodd. The path leads to Watson's Dodd. A simple climb reaches the northern cairn, the mid and the highest point of Stybarrow Dodd.

Make an easy descent west to a grassy col. The shoulder rises, to a bouldery top and cairn marking the White Stones top of Green Side. The next cairn offers a better view. Bear left and rise to the bouldery top of Hart Side. Proceed along the grassy heights. Bear right then left to the cairn and name plaque, which marks the top of Birkett Fell. Descend and follow the line of a ruined stone wall until a gap leads out onto the grassy shoulder of Brown Hills. Pass a couple of rocky knolls to gain the top of Brown Hills. Proceed to the rocky knoll and cairn of Swineside Knott. Cross the boggy expanse of Watermillock Common to ascend the final top of the round, Common Fell. Beyond the summit cairn of Common Fell stands a balanced rock of green stone. Pass it, then descend by the left bank of Blake Sike. Cross the latter halfway and descend to the fir plantation. Just to the right, pass through the gate in the wall and follow the fence above the river until an opening allows a descent to the footbridge. Cross Aira Beck then bear right across the field to a lane. At its top bear right, through a gate, turn left onto the road past Crookwath. Climb the road, passing the high wall and building of 'Penrith RDC Waterworks 1932'.

BRACKEN HOW, 1234FT/373M; ROUND HOW, 1207FT/387M

Maps: OS OL5, L90: GR 393211, GR 392208
Access point: Old quarry car park beside the A5091 on Park Brow, GR 397211
Distance/ascent: 3³/₄ mls/1330ft, 6km/405m
Approx time: 2 hours

Leave the old quarry car park by an overgrown path on its right side. Pass an old ruined building and climb a stile. Ascend steeply along the line of the wall until a further stile climbs the wall to the right. Follow the wall until the going levels. Bear right, picking the best route through the bracken, over little rocky ridges and two little green valleys. In the middle of a rocky-edged basin of grass stands a rocky knoll and slight cairn. Just above to the west a grassy mound marks the highest point of aptly named Bracken How.

Descend the shoulder into the bracken before ascending the more open flanks of Round How. Descend to the stone wall and bear right into a dip. Ascend steeply by the wall until it levels and turns a corner. Follow along the wall, in part now replaced by a fence and pass beneath Swineside Knott. Further on the path traverses the green scree tumbling down the face of Brown Hills. A narrow opening through the wall marks the top of the path which makes a diagonal descent through Glencoyne Park. Follow the path through thick woods of mature beech to a stile over the wall. Continue over Groovegill Beck. The path is now quite narrow and boggy. At its end a stile leads onto the A5091 opposite the high National Trust car park for Aira Force.

GLENRIDDING DODD, 1450FT/442M; HERON PIKE (GLENRIDDING), 2008FT/612M; SHEFFIELD PIKE, 2215FT/675M

Maps: OS OL5, L90: GR 381176, GR 374178, 369182
Access point: Glenridding car park, GR 386169
Distance/ascent: 5mls/1920ft, 8km/585m
Approx time: 3¼ hours

From the car park take the road rising through the centre of Glenridding village, past the Traveller's Rest Inn. Continue past the cottages on the right to a cattle grid. Beyond is another row of cottages but to the right a grassy track zigzags up the hillside. Follow this until, just before the cottages by an electricity pole and small scree, a small path rises steeply up to the right through bracken to a levelling behind a rocky knoll. This is the top of Blaes Crag. Bear left, following a path known as The Rake and ascend a grassy col. In front there is a stone wall and an opening that was once gated. Bear right along it and follow it around the corner. A path ascends the easy shoulder to the right. Go round the initial hump and on to a large cairn marking the top of Glenridding Dodd.

Return to the col and rise with the line of the wall. Make a scrambly ascent up the initial rocky knoll of the south-east ridge of Sheffield Pike. Where the path levels bear right to the grassy top and little cairn of Heron Pike. Regain the path and follow this to the summit cairn of Sheffield Pike. Descend the easy shoulder to the deep groove of Nick Head and turn right along the path which rises through it. Follow the well-defined path making a diagonal ascent above Glencoyne. Pass a broken dam, straddling Glencoyne Beck to skirt along a stone wall. Take a stile and enter the woods above Seldom Seen. Pass the cottages and continue along the track to the road and return to Glenridding.

23 HELVELLYN MASSIF

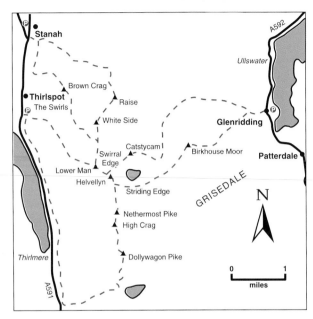

Location: Between Thirlmere to the west and Ullswater to the east, Central Fells.

Suggested Bases: Thirlmere and Ullswater.

Accommodation: Thirlmere: Youth hostel; b&b at the King's Head Inn; camping at Bridge End Farm and Dale Bottom. Bus service from Ambleside to Keswick. *Ullswater:* self-catering and b&b; Brotherswater and Traveller's Rest inns; Patterdale and Helvellyn youth hostels; Swirral camping barn above Glenridding; camping at Sykeside by Brotherswater, Side Farm in Patterdale, various sites above Watermillock and east of the lake are to be found Park Foot, Hill Crest and Waterside House; bus service from Penrith to Patterdale and Penrith to Keswick.

RAISE, 2897FT/883M; WHITE SIDE, 2832FT/863M; LOWER MAN on HELVELLYN, 3033FT/925M; HELVELLYN, 3118FT/950M; BROWN CRAG, 2001FT/610M

Maps: OS OL5, L90: GR 343174, GR 338167, GR 338155, GR 342151, GR 328177

Access point: Limited parking by telephone kiosk in the centre of
Stanah, GR 318189
Distance/ascent: 7½ mls/3200ft, 12km/975m
Approx time: 4½ hours

From the square ascend the surfaced road following the sign
'Bridleway Glenridding Via Sticks Pass'. Beside a barn on the
left, a stile leads over a stone wall. Take the next stile and
cross the aqueduct as it enters a section of tunnel. Shortly, a little
gate gives access to a bridge across Stanah Gill. Climb steeply to
the right of the gill. Soon the path enters a well-worn groove and
the angle slackens. Where the remains of an old stone structure
stand to the right the path bears left and moves into a high grassy
basin. Climb from the basin onto the shoulder on the right and
ascend this before cutting diagonally right towards Sticks Gill. Rise
from the head of the gill to a broad grassy col and the summit of
Sticks Pass. The main path now traverses along the spine of these
Central Fells. Follow the deeply grooved path up a little bouldery
scree to Raise. A cairn stands on the highest rocky turret.
Continue to the broad grassy rump of White Side and its summit
cairn.

Descend to the col and make a steep, rough ascent to the top
of Lower Man. A little stony descent and ascent up the edge of the
shoulder leads to the edge of the summit plateau above Swirral
Edge. Follow the curving edge past the trig point with a
spectacular view down to Red Tarn. Continue to the summit cairn
of Helvellyn beyond. Beneath this find the crossed walls of the
summit shelter. Retrace your steps to Lower Man and down to the
col beneath the north ridge. Bear left immediately on a vague path,
to find a well-defined path which skirts the western flanks of White
Side to allow the minor ascent of the rocky outcrop of Brown Crag

THE SUMMIT OF RAISE

to be made. Finally the path steepens and leads down through the bracken to a path which traverses above the stone wall. Bear right, following the path above the wall to cross Fisherplace Gill on a wooden footbridge. Follow the path to cross the next gill, that of Stanah at the foot of Sticks Pass.

BIRKHOUSE MOOR, 2356FT/718M; HELVELLYN, 3118FT/950M; CATSTYCAM, 2919FT/890M

Maps: OS OL5, L90: GR 364160, GR 342151, GR 348158
Access point: Glenridding car park, GR 386169
Distance/ascent: 7¹/₂ mls/3000ft, 12km/915m
Approx time: 4¹/₂ hours

Walk through Glenridding following the road to the junction at the bend. Bear left to cross Glenridding Beck by Rattlebeck Bridge. Pass the caravan site and continue on the track through the fell wall. Follow the path, bearing left to cross Mires Beck and make an ascent up Little Cove to a stone wall running down the shoulder above. The path follows the wall to the boggy ridge of Birkhouse Moor. The undistinguished highest point lies by the stone wall to the left. Cross it and proceed to the rocky end cone of Striding Edge, rightly called High Spying How. Follow the exposed crest of Striding Edge. At its end the going steepens, though there is little difficulty. Pass the Gough Memorial and follow the path to the summit shelter and the cairned highest point of Helvellyn. Follow the curving rim of the summit plateau past the trig point to the top of Swirral Edge.

The path plunges steeply though the going eases rapidly after the first section of descent. Continue along the ridge to the col then ascend to the top of Catstycam. Descend down the east ridge. The path is vague in places but soon joins the main highway in the vicinity of Red Tarn Beck. Follow the path down into the head of Glenridding. Cross Red Tarn Beck by a little footbridge. Continue above Glenridding Beck and cross it by a footbridge. Proceed down the track, passing the old mine buildings (now a youth hostel) to the Greenside Road. Pass the Traveller's Rest Inn to the car park.

LOWER MAN on HELVELLYN, 3033FT/925M; HELVELLYN, 3118FT/950M; NETHERMOST PIKE, 2922FT/891M; HIGH CRAG (GRISEDALE), 2903FT/885M; DOLLYWAGON PIKE, 2815FT/858M

Maps: OS OL5, L90: GR 338155, GR 342151, GR 344142,
   GR 343137, GR 346131
Access point: NWWA car park by the side of the A595, above
   Thirlspot, GR 317169
Distance/ascent: 9mls/2675ft, 14.5km/815m
Approx time: 4³/₄ hours

STRIDING EDGE

Follow the path from the back of the large car park to rise up the flanks of Helvellyn by the side of Helvellyn Gill. The going steepens as you climb over the end of Browncove Crags. The angle slackens and the path continues above the crags until it is possible to bear left and bag the top of Lower Man. Descend to the col beneath and follow the main trod directly to the summit cairn of Helvellyn. Follow the main trod south past the shelter. Bear right across the broad shoulder of Helvellyn to reach a low point and junction with the eastern edge of the plateau, overlooking Nethermost Cove. Just beyond, the trod divides. First take the left fork, then leave the main path to follow the eastern edge along to the summit cairn of Nethermost Pike. Proceed across the summit, striking a line south to regain the eastern edge of the massif.

Ascend to the large summit cairn of High Crag. Proceed south along the eastern edge, first falling then rising again to a cairned bump on the flank of Dollywagon Pike. The summit lies a little further on. A cairned grassy dome, narrowing to the east, marks the highest point of Dollywagon Pike, though the rise to its west bears the major cairn. Join the main trod that lies below to the south. Descend the zigzags to Grisedale Tarn. The head of Grisedale Pass leads to Grasmere with the Fairfield Group above. Follow the path above the shores of the tarn, cross the line of the old boundary fence and proceed down the southern side of Raise Beck. Just above the pass of Dunmail Raise a gate leads through the wall on the right. The path leads to a footbridge over Birkside Gill. Continue along the level track and make an easy return through the conifer woods above Thirlmere. Walk over Whelpside Gill above Wythburn Church and cross a footbridge over an unnamed gill. Continue until a slight descent leads back to the car park.

24 FAIRFIELD GROUP

Location: North of the head of Windermere Lake, Central Fells.
Suggested Bases: Ambleside, Grasmere and Ullswater.
Accommodation: Ambleside: all facilities except railway station
and campsite. Ambleside (Waterhead) youth hostel.
Grasmere: plentiful accommodation though limited facilities.
No railway station and no campsite. Butterlip Howe and
Thorney How youth hostels. *Ullswater:* self-catering and b&b;
Brotherswater and Traveller's Rest inns; Patterdale and
Helvellyn youth hostels; Swirral camping barn above
Glenridding; camping at Sykeside by Brotherswater, Side
Farm in Patterdale, various sites above Watermillock and east
of the lake are to be found Park Foot, Hill Crest and
Waterside House; bus service from Penrith to Patterdale and
Penrith to Keswick.

ARNISON CRAG, 1422FT/433M; BIRKS, 2040FT/622M; GAVEL PIKE,
2572FT/784M; ST SUNDAY CRAG, 2758FT/841M; COFA PIKE,
2700FT/823M; FAIRFIELD, 2863FT/873M; HART CRAG, 2698FT/822M; GILL
CRAG on HARTSOP ABOVE HOW, 1909FT/582M; GALE CRAG,
1680FT/512M

Maps: OS OL5, L90: GR 394150, GR 380143, GR 373134,
GR 369134, 359121, GR 359118, GR 369112, GR 383120,
GR 392124
Access point: Car park (fee charged) on the opposite side of the
A592 to the Patterdale Hotel, GR 396159
Distance/ascent: 9¹/2 mls/3495ft, 15km/1065m
Approx time: 5¹/4 hours

Pass the right end of the Patterdale Hotel to find a footpath
which leads to a kissing gate through a wire fence. A broad
path rises through bracken and over a bump to descend to a
gate through a stone wall. Don't pass through the gate but bear left
following the side of the stone wall as it ascends the hillside,
passing Oxford Crag to the left. As the wall levels and turns a
corner a path continues the ascent to the left. Follow this to a level
shoulder, then ascend steeply left to a corridor. This runs to the
north of Arnison Crag. A little rocky step-up leads to the summit.
Regain the shoulder and continue along the path which bears left
but then swings back right towards a mound. Either go over this or
go round it to the right. Take a central course through the grassy
hollows and hummocks to find the grassy corridor of Trough
Head. Cross it at its head and ascend the shoulder which rises
beyond. Gradually curve to the right. In a hollow beneath a craggy
outcrop pass a little stone structure before gaining the ruinous line
of an ancient stone wall. Ascend the line of the wall, continuing in
the same direction when it peters out, to gain the path cresting the
shoulder above. This leads to the flat grassy top of Birks. An

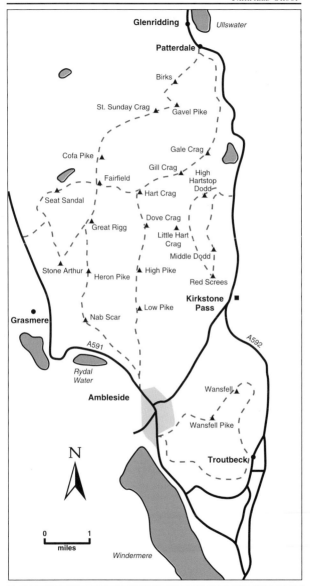

unspectacular top yet one that offers fine views. Continue along the grassy shoulder past slate outcrops. Gain the main trod which rises from Grisedale to St Sunday Crag directly in front. After a short section of ascent a well-defined path bears off left for a comfortable diagonal climb to Gavel Pike. The path back along the shoulder continues in a short way to the summit cairn which marks the rocky top of St Sunday Crag. A long shoulder falls to the col of Deepdale Hause. The ascent appears to be formidable yet proves reasonably straightforward. Nearing the top, boulder balances upon boulder and there is a little scramble before a grassy, broken rock edge topped by a cairn. This is the summit of Cofa Pike. The path continues to traverse a rocky point beyond, before beginning the ascent of the final flanks of Fairfield. The path splits, the left fork giving the steepest but most direct ascent to the summit shelters of Fairfield. The summit plateau of Fairfield is rather flat and featureless. A proliferation of cairns and the meeting of four major routes also make it notoriously treacherous to navigate correctly in poor visibility. Pass the most northerly shelter to find another large stone shelter, 20m to the south. At this point bear left, to follow the northern rim of the plateau across the head of a gully known as Flinty Grave. Once located the path becomes well defined and leads along the spine of the mountain.

Descend slightly past the head of Scrubby Crag before making a steep rocky descent to Link Hause. Beyond the dip ascend directly up Hart Crag, bearing right at the top of the rise to find the long rocky summit crest marked by a cairn. Cross the main path and bear slightly left to find a path leading down to the long ridge of Hartsop above How. After a short way the path skirts the edge of Link Cove to the left. It then bears right to follow a central line down the nose. The path moves left, with a short rocky scramble down a rock slab, to a steep descent leading to the flatter ground below. Continue over Blake Brow through peat hags and bogs until a short ascent leads to the top of Gill Crag on Hartsop above How. Descend the shoulder through a corridor to follow a stone wall before rising again to the definite summit of Gale Crag with its little rocky tops. Follow the wall and then squeeze through a narrow corridor to descend the ridge. Cross the wall which rises from the left, by a stile, then follow the path to the left. The path leads down the broadening shoulder into the woods of Deepdale Park. Enter the woods until after a little way the path splits. Bear left to a stile over a wall and an old barn. Follow the permissive path to a track. This leads onto the main road by the telephone kiosk at Deepdale Bridge near Bridgend. Follow the road to Patterdale.

MIDDLE DODD, 2146FT/654M; RED SCREES, 2545FT/776M; WEST TOP of LITTLE HART CRAG, 2091FT/637M; HIGH HARTSOP DODD, 1702FT/519M

Maps: OS OL5, OL7, L90: GR 397095, GR 397088, GR 387100, GR 393108

Access point: Lay-by on the Hartsop side of Kirkstone Pass, GR 402113

Distance/ascent: 5¼ mls/2933ft, 8.5km/894m
Approx time: 3½ hours

 A short distance along the road a stile (signposted 'Public Footpath') leads into the field. Strike a diagonal line across this until, above a barn to the right, a further sign points to a wooden bridge over Kirkstone Beck. Beyond this a stile crosses the wall (note the footbridge over Caiston Beck to the right. This will be used on the return). A vague path leads up to the ruined fell wall. Ascending steeply follow the line of the wall up and across the flanks of Middle Dodd, keeping with the wall as it levels. Where the wall drops over a little crag, it is best to ascend directly up the nose of the fell. The path becomes better defined as the ascent progresses. Nearing the top it bears right before rising to the summit cairn of Middle Dodd. Walk past a hollow to a saddle. Cross the old wall to climb Smallthwaite Band, which contours around the rim of the rocky combe below. The going eases and the trig point and summit cairn of Red Screes are gained.
Circumnavigate the summit tarn and continue until a well-defined path splits down to the right from the rocky plateau. Cross a large rock slab near the bottom and follow the line of the wall which falls to the head of Scandale Pass. Cross the pass and ascend again, still following the wall until it turns left and is joined by a fence.

Our way lies to the right of Scandale Tarn. Ascend by the line of the fence until the path bears off right. It climbs to the shoulder west of Little Hart Crag. Climb to the first and highest top, which is the West Top of Little Hart Crag. Cross to the second top, which is more shapely though lower, before finding an easy descent down to the left. A grassy shoulder leads easily down to the final cairned grassy bump which is taken to be the summit of High Hartsop Dodd. Plunge steeply down the nose of the fell, following the well-defined path. Before the barn bear right. Follow the path through a gate in the wall. Walk along the flanks of the fell above the wall, until the path rises from the wall. After a little way, before a kissing gate, a path bears down to the left to the footbridge over Caiston Beck.

LOW PIKE, 1667FT/508M; HIGH PIKE on SCANDALE FELL, 2152FT/656M; DOVE CRAG, 2598FT/792M; HART CRAG, 2698FT/822M; FAIRFIELD, 2863FT/873M; GREAT RIGG, 2513FT/766M; RYDAL FELL, 2037FT/621M; HERON PIKE (RYDAL), 2008FT/612M; NAB SCAR, 1450FT/442M

Maps: OS OL5, OL7, L90: GR 348093, GR 374088, GR 375105, GR 369112, GR 359118, GR 356104, GR 357087, GR 356083, GR 356071
Access point: Ambleside, the Rydal Road car park, GR 376046
Distance/ascent: 10¼ mls/3430ft, 16.5km/1045m
Approx time: 6 hours

 Bear right and cross the road to ascend the Kirkstone Road for a short distance only, before Nook Lane rises off to the left (the Golden Rule pub lies higher to the right). Follow the Nook

Lane to Nook Farm. The track continues across Low Sweden
Bridge before rising through the fields. Above the fields the main
path bears right. An alternative to this follows the crest by the
wall, rejoining the main trod a little further on by the craggy little
scar of High Brock Crag. Thereafter the main path follows the
stone wall. Low Pike has a cairned top and should not be missed
by taking the path to its right. Next comes the gentler height of
High Pike followed by the summit of Dove Crag. A descent and a
slight ascent lead to the stony ridged top of Hart Crag. A steep dip
into Link Hause is followed by a very stony ascent. The angle eases
and the path leads rapidly up onto the summit plateau of Fairfield.
The central circular shelter cairn is the best resting place on this
walk. Head initially east, then go south to find the plunge down
the western leg of the horseshoe. Dip over Calf Cove and ascend to
the cairned top of Great Rigg (sometimes called Greatrigg Man).
Plunge over the undulations of Rydal Fell to its summit and carry
on to Heron Pike. Nab Scar, prominently cairned, soon follows.
Bear left following the path until it intercepts the track which rises
from the hamlet of Rydal. Descend the surfaced road past Rydal
Mount, the final home of William Wordsworth. A track bears off to
the left. This passes above Rydal Hall and across Rydal Beck by a
stone-arched bridge. A lovely return through Rydal Park leads to
the A591 just outside of Ambleside.

SEAT SANDAL, 2415FT/736M; FAIRFIELD, 2863FT/873M; GREAT RIGG,
2513FT/766M; STONE ARTHUR, 1652FT/504M

Maps: OS OL5, L90: GR 344115, GR 359118, GR 356104,
    GR 374078
Access point: Grasmere, verge parking by the side of the A591 at
    the junction with minor road to Low Mill Bridge, GR 335091
Distance/ascent: 6½ mls/2805ft, 10km/855m
Approx time: 3½ hours

Opposite the junction a lane, signposted 'Public Bridleway
Patterdale' leads up past the houses. The lane opens to
Tongue Gill on the right and continues past a gate and barn on
the left. Continue up the lane to the confluence of Little Tongue
Gill and Tongue Gill. Cross the first footbridge and follow the
track which rises up to the left, with the spur of Great Tongue
above to the right. The track crosses the stream to a gate. Bear
right following the line of the wall. Stay with the wall as it swings
left. Follow a path that leads horizontally left through the bracken,
across the flank of the fell onto the long southerly nose of Seat
Sandal. Ascend steeply and continue to a grassy rise. The route
continues to make a grinding ascent until the angle eases and the
path becomes less well-defined. Keep in the same line past cairns
and continue over the summit plateau to the substantial cairn of
Seat Sandal. Cross the wall and descend east to Grisedale Hause.
Cross the Grisedale Pass packhorse route and climb along the line
of the ruined stone wall up the scree flanks of Fairfield zigzaging to

gain the stony summit plateau of Fairfield. First move east then leave the summit due south. Descend then ascend the shoulder to Great Rigg. Follow the main trod over the initial rocky top of Great Rigg until a grassy path swings off to the right. This leads down the spur to gain the rocky castle of Stone Arthur (also known as Arthur's Seat). A path takes a slight corridor through this rock outcrop. The highest point is a cairned rock to its left. Bear right, above the cliffs. Descend to Brackenwife Knotts. Continue down the fellside to the line of the stone wall. Follow this to the old packhorse track just above Tongue Gill cross the gills by the footbridges and return.

WANSFELL PIKE, 1588FT/484M; WANSFELL, 1597FT/487M

Maps: OS OL7, L90: GR 394042, GR 404053
Access point: Ambleside, Fisherbeck car park by the side of the
    Windermere Road, GR 377038
Distance/ascent: 6³/₄ mls/1875ft, 11km/570m
Approx time: 3¹/₂ hours

Leave the back of the car park and turn left along the road. At the first junction walk uphill to the right. Follow this road and bear left to a junction with the Blue Hill road. Continue up this to a walled lane leading up and left across the flanks of the fell. Continue along the track until it meets the main path which rises directly up the slopes of Wansfell. Follow the well defined path which steepens at the top and winds leftwards up the rocky summit knoll of Wansfell Pike. Take the stile just beyond the summit and continue along the undulating spine of the fell. A stile over the second wall gives access to the grassy summit of Wansfell. The path follows the line of the wall, towards Troutbeck, to intercept Nanny Lane. The Lane leads directly into Troutbeck Village. Proceed to the right towards the post office, which offers home-made teas. Immediately beyond the PO follow the track, Robin Lane, which rises to the right. Continue rising to the right until a signposted path bears off horizontally to the left. Follow this to High Skelghyll and continue along the track through Skelgyhll Wood descending to gain the road a short way from the car park.

25 LOADPOT HILL GROUP

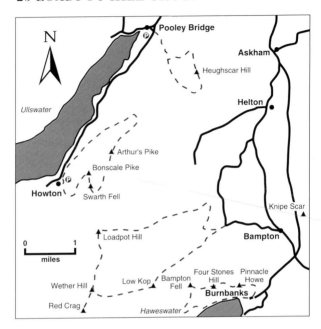

Location: Between the bottoms of Ullswater and Haweswater,
Eastern Fells.

Suggested Bases: Ullswater, Penrith and Lowther.

Accommodation: *Ullswater:* self-catering and b&b; Brotherswater
and Traveller's Rest inns; Patterdale and Helvellyn youth
hostels; Swirral camping barn above Glenridding; camping at
Sykeside by Brotherswater, Side Farm in Patterdale, various
sites above Watermillock and east of the lake are to be found
Park Foot, Hill Crest and Waterside House; bus service from
Penrith to Patterdale and Penrith to Keswick. *Penrith:* all
facilities except youth hostel and camping. *Lowther:* self-
catering and b&b; several inns to be found in Askham,
Helton, Shap and Bampton; no youth hostels, no bus service.

HEUGHSCAR HILL, 1231FT/375M

Maps: OS OL5, L90: GR 488232

Access point: Pooley Bridge, public car parks on either side of the
bridge, GR 471244

Distance/ascent: 4¼ mls/740ft, 7km/225m
Approx time: 1¾ hours

 Through the village centre take the Howtown road past the church. Cross the main road at the junction. Continue in the same direction and rise with the road until it becomes a track. Follow this rising up the flanks of the hill. A cairn marks the position where the High Street Roman road descends from Loadpot Hill crossing our track to traverse the flanks of Heughscar Hill. Continue straight on past a boundary stone and path bearing off left. Rise with the path to the left. Keep the plantation to the right and climb to the summit plateau of Heughscar Hill. Pass the distinct Boundary Stone and continue to the cairn that marks the top of Heughscar Hill. Take the path descending to the north, crossing above the limestone outcrop of Heugh Scar, before gaining a track. Bear left, cross the Roman road, and descend to the corner of a wall. Bear right by the wall to gain the original track taken in ascent.

ARTHUR'S PIKE, 1747FT/532M; SWARTH FELL (ULLSWATER), 1788FT/545M; BONSCALE PIKE, 1718FT/524M

Maps: OS OL5, L90: GR 461207, GR 454195, GR 453201
Access point: Howtown, limited parking at the public launching site, GR 444199 or arrive by steamer from either Glenridding or Pooley Bridge (summer service only)
Distance/ascent: 5½ mls/1440ft, 9km/440m.
Approx time: 3 hours

 Cross the road to a metal gate and signpost 'Public Footpath, Pooley Bridge, Askham'. Rise through the field to exit via a garden gate on the left. Leave the garden by steps and a gate to the right. Gain the track running above the fell wall. Pass beneath the crags of Bonscale Pike. Continue along by the wall over the bridge over Swarthbeck Gill. Continue along the track until, after a barn, the track splits. Bear right and rise diagonally up the hillside; signed 'Moor Divock, Helton'. Cross boggy ground either side of a covered reservoir and rise above the edge of the wood of Barton Park. Here a path bears off right from the track and climbs a sward of grass directly up the hillside. Follow this to the shoulder then follow the grassy trod on the right, to the top of White Knott. Continue along the slight path, which runs along this Ullswater edge of Barton Fell, past another cairned knoll on the right. Rise to a cairn then bear right out to the cairn on Loup Knott. Follow the path traversing rightwards to a stone cairn which stands below Arthur's Pike. Climb the hill behind to a cairned knoll marking the summit of Arthur's Pike. Beyond can be seen the High Street Roman road. Follow the vague path towards it, then bear right to intercept a grassy track falling from it towards the hollow of Swarth Gill. Cross the beck then ascend to the left over boggy ground to find the boggy table top summit of

Swarth Fell. Bear right and descend the grassy shoulder to a col. As you ascend again, a grooved grassy track will be observed on the left edge. Follow the track to a cairn on the summit of Bonscale Pike. A path traverses to the right, above the old track, across steep hillside to the lower rectangular masonry pillar known as Bonscale Tower. Above stands another 'tower' of rather inferior construction. Above this there's a further smaller cairn. Rise to the higher tower. Find to its north an ancient path, which descends steeply to meet the zigzag elbow of the track that ran past Bonscale Pike. This track runs diagonally down the hillside, below the crags of Bonscale Pike. Follow it until a path bears off left, traversing to the easier ground of the shoulder which stands above the bay of Howtown Wyke. Keep bearing left across it to find a grooved track, falling from above, which continues to make a diagonal ascent left across the slopes of the hillside. Midway down the slope a track/path cuts off to the right and this descends to the fell wall. Bear right to find the gate into the garden.

LOW KOP, 1877FT/572M; RED CRAG, 2333FT/711M; WETHER HILL, 2205FT/672M; LOADPOT HILL, 2201FT/671M

Maps: OS OL5, L90: GR 472165, GR 450152, GR 456168, GR 457181

Access point: Limited verge parking on the road below Moorahill Farm, GR 495182

Distance/ascent: 8¾ mls/1540ft, 14km/470m

Approx time: 3¾ hours

A grassy path follows the wall, south of the road, to continue across open ground before falling to a stone-slab bridge across Cawdale Beck. Rise steeply onto the plateau past the circle of Towtop Kirk. The path continues across the grassy plateau to join a well-defined track which rises up Hause End. The track levels passing numerous knolls before passing between two plantations either side of the nose. Pass a cairn to the left and continue with the track to Low Kop. Continue along the centre of the shoulder and rise again to the levelling of High Kop. Make a level traverse out onto the shoulder. Continue to the main track and path of the High Street Roman road. The independent top of Red Crag lies up to the left. Descend left to the col, then rise with the track through the gap in the wall up onto Red Crag. A fence stands to the right. A large cairn and post stand centrally just to the west of the fence which is holed at this point. The highest point is an uncairned grassy bump just to the south.

Join the High Street Roman road and follow it back down to the col. Continue up the first grassy top of Wether Hill and continue to the next, the most northerly of which is taken to be the summit. The summit cairn of Wether Hill lies just above the track/path. Continue along High Street, descending to the col, then ascending the grassy hillside beyond. Pass ruined Lowther House. The path leads to the stone trig point of Loadpot Hill. Find the

APPROACHING PINNACLE HOWE FROM BURNBANKS

grassy path heading due east and follow it, making an easy and rapid descent down Hart Hill. A length of ancient stone wall on the left, marked as 'Bield' on the OS map, is joined and a track enters from the right which is followed in descent. It leads left across the boggy expanse of The Pen. As the track winds down Pen End, above a coppice of trees behind the fell wall, bear right along the path above the wall. Pass a barn and down to Carhullan Farm. A gated lane leads through the farm to the surfaced road below Moorahill Farm.

PINNACLE HOWE, 1257FT/383M; FOUR STONES HILL, 1362FT/415M; BAMPTON FELL, 1604FT/489M

Maps: OS OL5, L90: GR 497167, GR 492163, GR 487165
Access point: In the hamlet of Burnbanks, beneath Haweswater Dam. Either park at the end of the road opposite the houses (do not obstruct local parking) in the centre or by the locked gate on the track that continues along the northern shore. A track is signed 'MCWW Public Footpath' leading off right from the road, GR 506161
Distance/ascent: 4¼ mls/1180ft, 7km/360m
Approx time: 2¼ hours

Follow the track through the bungalows and wood, rising to a locked gate and stile. Beyond the stile bear right along a grassy trod which cuts through the bracken. The track crosses another and traverses the hillside before making an ascent. To the right of the Aika Sike stream, stands the gorse-covered Aika Hill and a well-defined track. Bear right to this track and follow it behind Drybarrows Farm. Bear left to climb the angular grassy mound of Pinnacle Howe. Descend to the west across the low boggy area via a prominent mound. Continue straight up the flanks of Birkhouse Hill. Head south, picking a route over the numerous grassy hummocks to a view over Haweswater on the edge of the plateau. Beyond, on the flanks of Four Stones Hill stands a prominent cairn. Make a steep scramble to the top of Four Stones Hill. Climb directly up the hillside beyond to cross a track, rising from Drybarrows. Rise to the cairned top of Bampton Fell (unnamed on the OS map). Descend the shoulder aiming for a cairn on a rocky knoll. The track crossed previously, runs beneath the cairn. Cross it again to work directly down the flanks of the hill to the track that passed behind Four Stones Hill. It leads to a wooden footbridge over Measand Beck. Don't cross the bridge but bear left along a path which falls to the main track above the eastern shore of Haweswater.

KNIPE SCAR, 1122FT/342M

Maps: OS OL5, L90: GR 526191
Access point: Limited verge parking beyond the cattle grid leading onto the open ground of Knipe Moor, GR 521187
Distance/ascent: 3mls/500ft, 5km/150m
Approx time: 1¼ hours

A path, signposted 'Public Footpath' leads off to the right and crosses the moor. It rises to turn right and follow along the fell wall. The track rises to old lime kilns and quarries but the path takes the stile in front over the wall. The signposted path continues to traverse the hillside, before bearing left to rise past Low Scarside onto Knipescar Common. Turn left and walk along the rim of the scar. At the most prominent point of the scar the rim slopes inwards. A sunken circular trig point marks the top of Knipe Scar. Proceeding north the scar diminishes and a way can be found down onto the shoulder below. A green swathe path of grass cuts through the bracken down the hillside. It crosses a hollow and rises before finally falling back to the road.

26 BRANSTREE GROUP

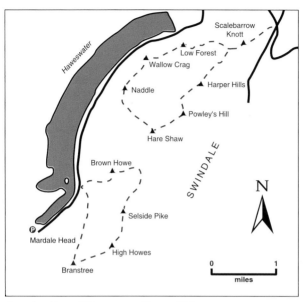

Location: East of Haweswater, Eastern Fells.

Suggested Bases: Ullswater, Penrith and Lowther.

Accommodation: Ullswater: self-catering and b&b; Brotherswater and Traveller's Rest inns; Patterdale and Helvellyn youth hostels; Swirral camping barn above Glenridding; camping at Sykeside by Brotherswater, Side Farm in Patterdale, various sites above Watermillock and east of the lake are to be found Park Foot, Hill Crest and Waterside House; bus service from Penrith to Patterdale and Penrith to Keswick. *Penrith:* all facilities except youth hostel and camping. *Lowther:* self-catering and b&b; several inns to be found in Askham, Helton, Shap and Bampton; no youth hostels; no bus service.

SCALEBARROW KNOTT, 1109FT/338M; HARPER HILLS, 1375FT/419M; POWLEY'S HILL, 1526FT/465M; HARE SHAW, 1650FT/503M; NADDLE HIGH FOREST, 1427FT/435M; WALLOW CRAG, 1421FT/433M; NADDLE LOW FOREST, 1398FT/426M

Maps: OS OL5, L90: GR 519152, GR 510144, GR 505135, GR 498131, GR 492143, GR 496149, GR 502150

Access point: Track from concrete NWWA road just above the junction with the Rosgill to Swindale road, GR 526157

Distance/ascent: 6¾ mls/1706ft, 11km/520m
Approx time: 3½ hours

The track leads quickly to the heights of Scalebarrow Knott. Bear right at the division and then right again from the track, the second cairned grassy dome is the highest. Regain the track and follow it up Harper Hills. To the right nearing the top is the NWWA reservoir/pumping station and above, to the left, a cairned knoll. This is taken as the representative top for Harper Hills. Beyond, pick a route between the numerous grassy knolls, before bearing right back to the track. Take the gate through the fence line and continue beneath the flanks of Powley's Hill. Ascend directly up the hillside, clipping the left edge of the bracken, to find the highest point. It appears to be a bouldery outcrop on the north-east edge of the summit area, though the OS indicates a point to the south. Undulating terrain leads to a rise holding two standing stones. The next objective is the cairned shoulder, indicated on the OS, which extends eastwards from the heights of Hare Shaw. Intervening below there's a flat boggy hollow which is best circumnavigated by its left edge.

Pass a small chambered mound before rising over rough and sometimes boggy ground to the summit cairn of Hare Shaw on the knoll. The OS indicates that a rise to the south is actually the highest point. Descend from here, picking the best route through the brackened knolls and flat bogs before ascending a shoulder and falling to the stone wall. Follow it to the left. Cross the col and make a short descent to a hurdle gate. Walk through this and go right over another hurdle gate to find a track traversing left across Naddle High Forest. At a fence gate bear left and ascend directly to the bilberry and heather top of Naddle High Forest. It is probably best to continue along the undulating rim, with sections of thick bracken and heather, directly towards the next prominent top of Wallow Crag. This cairned top stands beyond a wire fence, which must be climbed. Beyond lies the raised edge of Naddle Low Forest. Bear right, south, descending to a wooden fence. Stride this and walk down rough pasture to the head of a track. This falls in turn to a further track, which is followed through extensive woods of alder to a junction above Naddle Farm. Bear right, through a gate and stile, to cross Naddle Beck by the ford. A gate and stile above to the right lead to a track which is followed through the woods to a gate. Through the gate the track opens out. Rise to a gate in the fell wall. Bear left along the shoulder and once more crest Scalebarrow Knott.

BRANSTREE, 2339FT/713M; HIGH HOWES (MARDALE), 2208FT/673M; SELSIDE PIKE, 2149FT/655M; BROWN HOWE (MARDALE), 1736FT/529M

Maps: OS OL5, L90: GR 478100, GR 488103, GR 491112, GR 487122
Access point: Lay-by/verge by the Hawseswater road, GR 480118
Distance/ascent: 4¾ mls/1755ft, 7.5km/535m
Approx time: 2½ hours

RUINED BUILDINGS ON THE FLANKS OF BRANSTREE WITH HAWESWATER BELOW

A little gate over the bridge gives access to Branstree's north ridge. A path leads up to the right out of the gill, zigzagging steeply. Pass beneath the large boulder with a cavernous base, named Hollow Stone. Continue past two ruined stone buildings to gain the easier angled grassy shoulder above. Head directly up the shoulder to the broad flat grassy summit plateau. A circular basin trig point and little cairn mark the summit. A grassy path leads out to an airier perch; the rocky shoulder of Artlecrag Pike. Descend, bearing right to the fence line and stride over it to pass an old masonry survey tower. Pass the little tarn on a grassy neck. Continue up the tuffeted grass to the top of High Howes (unnamed on the OS map). Descend directly down the shoulder to meet the fenceline where it bends. Stride over this and continue to the cairn and shelter marking the top of Selside Pike. The pronounced shoulder of Selside End falls to the old corpse route. Make a grassy descent and swing left to the corpse road by an old wooden post. Follow the track towards Hawsewater, bearing right to ascend the cairned top of Brown Howe. Return to the track beneath Rowantreethwaite Well and descend through the zizags.

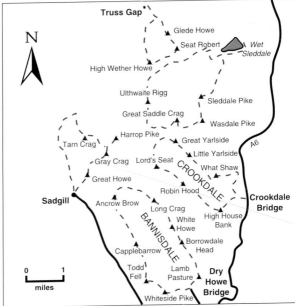

Location: West of the A6 Shap Road, Eastern Fells.
Suggested Bases: Penrith, Lowther and Kendal.
Accommodation: Penrith: all facilities except youth hostel and camping. *Lowther:* self-catering and b&b; several inns to be found in Askham, Helton, Shap and Bampton; no youth hostels; no bus service. *Kendal:* all facilities; Kendal youth hostel; no camping.

HIGH WETHER HOWE, 1742FT/531M; SEAT ROBERT, 1688FT/515M; GLEDE HOWE, 1562FT/476M

Maps: OS OL5, L90: GR 515109, GR 527114, GR 521120
Access point: Limited parking at Swindale, between the NWWA intake dam and the footbridge below Truss Gap Farm, GR 516132. The road up Swindale is extremely narrow and parking is encouraged where the open expanse of Rosgill Moor becomes a walled lane into Swindale, GR 521142. This lengthens the walk by 1½ mls/2.5km.
Distance/ascent: 4¼ mls/1165ft, 7km/355m
Approx time: 2 hours

Cross the bridge. Bear right to the track which rises through bracken. The track zigzags and bears left, away from the gill, before again bearing right to gain the plateau. An ancient cairn marks the top of Truss Gap. Bear right. Cross Haskew Beck above the little waterfall and continue along the fell wall. Cross a knoll and traverse beneath the west face of Beastman's Crag with its slatey rocks stacked like cards. Cross a boggy area and bear right onto the lower shoulder which falls from Fewling Stones. Climb the shoulder to the summit area. Continue easily along the undulating broad edge, a track will be found to the right, to gain the rocky knoll of High Wether Howe. A fence lies below. Bear left taking a line parallel to it but picking a higher, drier route through the boggy depressions. Seat Robert appears as a saddle in front. Climb its south hump to reach its higher northern dome. A high grassy shoulder falls north and this is followed to Glede Howe. There are two rocky knoll tops of apparently equal altitude. The first is larger, yet the second feels the most independent and a cairn stands upon a flat rock. Below to the right is a ruined bield. Observe ahead the cairn which marks the head of Truss Gap Pass. Head for it, passing a knoll with a rowan growing from its face. Avoid boggy ground and pick up the right side of Haskew Beck as it turns around the the corner of the fell wall. Pass the head of Gouthercrag Gill and return to Truss Gap.

SLEDDALE PIKE, 1659FT/506M; WASDALE PIKE, 1854FT/565M; GREAT SADDLE CRAG, 1850FT/564M; ULTHWAITE RIGG, 1647FT/502M

Maps: OS OL5, OL7, L90: GR 536094, GR 537085, GR 526086, GR 515093
Access point: Car park by Wet Sleddale Dam, GR 555114
Distance/ascent: 8½ mls/985ft, 14km/300m
Approx time: 3½ hours

Follow the track above Wet Sleddale Reservoir to the first building at New Ings. A vague path rises to the left to a gate through the fell wall. Follow Poorhag Gill to a track which terminates in a curious wooden structure known as the Lunch House. Continue the ascent by Howe Gill before traversing right to a large boulder of beautiful pink Shap granite known as the Gray Bull. Continue the rightwards traverse to the cairned summit of Sleddale Pike. Proceed to the cairned heights of Great Saddle Crag then take a circuitous route down to Ulthwaite Rigg. The bridleway falling from Mosedale is the next objective: cross the wet hollow to reach it. Bear right along the track until another track leaves it to fall through zigzags to Sleddale Hall. Pass the Hall and descend along the track to a footbridge across the beck. The way leads back via a further footbridge to New Ings.

HIGH HOUSE BANK, 1625FT/495M; ROBIN HOOD, 1617FT/493M; LORD'S
SEAT on HIGH HOUSE FELL, 1719FT/524M; GREAT YARLSIDE,
1952FT/595M; LITTLE YARLSIDE, 1691FT/516M; WHAT SHAW,
1593FT/485M

Maps: OS OL7, L90: GR 543048, GR 530059, GR 518066,
    GR 522079, GR 532072, GR 542061
Access point: Verge parking below Crookdale Bridge, GR 552055
Distance/ascent: 6³/₄ mls/1705ft, 11km/520m
Approx time: 3¹/₂ hours

From a point just beyond the old stone barn, climb the
hillside directly to the fell wall topped by a fence. Cross this
and bear left to the prominent cairn on the shoulder. Just
above the cairn is the grass and bilberry mound top of High House
Bank. Descend the shoulder, through the fence gate to gain the col.
Slightly boggy ground rises to a stone wall and gate. Beyond,
bearing slightly left, make a steep ascent to the grassy summit of
Robin Hood. There is a fine ancient cairn below to the west
standing prominently above Borrowdale. The going now improves
considerably as does the general ambience of the walk. Follow a
vague but satisfactory grassy track along the shoulder to the grassy
platform of Lord's Seat. It is slightly ridged to the south and this
must be regarded as the top: there is no cairn. Turn right, across
the head of Crookdale, through the peat hags, over three little
streams and above the stone walls of Crookdale Fold. A vague
grassy path rises steeply up the hillside to the right of the ravine
formed by the third stream. Cross a small rocky outcrop and gain
the easier grassy terrain of Lawyer's Brow before striking
rightwards to join a stone wall. Follow the wall, across the
indistinct summit of Great Yarlside to a grass mound on the right
of the wall. Descend along the shoulder until a gap in the wall leads
to the highest point of Little Yarlside. Descend on the right side of
the wall to the col. Rise again, taking the fence stile before bearing
right over rough ground which rises to a fine cairn on a ruined
wall. Rise with the old wall line to stride a fence and gain the
highest grassy top of What Shaw. Follow the fence to the left and
rise to the second lesser top of What Shaw. Descend to a fence.
Bear right to a track and follow it through the gate. Follow the
track which is joined by another from the right through the gates
to Crookdale Bridge Farm.

WHITESIDE PIKE, 1302FT/397M; TODD FELL, 1314FT/401M;
CAPPLEBARROW, 1681FT/512M; ANCHROW BROW, 1816FT/553M; LONG
CRAG on BANNISDALE FELL, 1617FT/493M; WHITE HOWE (BANNISDALE),
1737FT/530M; BORROWDALE HEAD, 1734FT/528M; LAMB PASTURE,
1205FT/367M

Maps: OS OL7, L90: GR 521015, GR 512021, GR 508035,
    GR 501055, GR 516052, GR 524042, GR 528036, GR 532021
Access point: Bannisdale: limited parking by the junction above
    Dryhowe Bridge, GR 531017
Distance/ascent: 8mls/2180ft, 13km/665m
Approx time: 4 hours

Above the road take the fence gate and head straight up the
hillside. Stride the fence and continue the ascent to a cairned
knoll. Bear right along the wall, until a stone stile crosses the
wall to the left. Bear left of the little tarn and climb to the cairned
knoll of Whiteside Pike. Take the path through heather, bearing
left to the hog-hole in the stone wall. Take the stone slab stile and
ascend the grassy flanks beyond to Todd Fell. Surmount the next
stone wall and progress along the shoulder until barred by a wire
fence. Stride the lesser fence to the right and pass a rocky knoll
which is joined by a further fence rising from Dub Ings Wood in
Bannisdale. Stride this and climb to the top of Capplebarrow. The
summit point is itself traversed by the fence. Fall down the grassy
shoulder beyond, taking the gate through a fence, before rising
again to pass a boggy tarn. Rise to a corner in the fence. A cairn
stands beyond it on the Longsleddale side, this is the highest top of
Ancrow Brow.

Follow the old wall around the grassy shoulder. From the
highest grassy point at the head of Bannisdale descend down the
shoulder. Cross boggy ground to a little rock outcrop. The bog
behind this is best circumnavigated to the right before an ascent
leads to a stile over the fence and gap in the ruined wall to the
knoll of Long Crag – Bannisdale Fell. Pick the best line over
uneven grassy terrain to cross the line of a ruined stone wall. Begin
ascending the grassy, heathery, peaty flanks of White Howe. Bear
right, away from the wall to a grass plateau capped by a concrete
trig point. This is the top of White Howe. Dip down to a col and
cross the fence by a stile and the ruinous wall by a gap to rise
again to the grassy top and little cairn of Borrowdale Head.
Descend the shoulder to a wet hollow. Follow down the left side of
a drainage ditch/stream, which is the source of Priest Gill, and
then bear left through the rushes to a gate in the stone wall. Take
the gate and climb directly to the grassy top of Lamb Pasture.
Make your way right to the edge of craggy ground. To the right a
grassy cleft leads steeply but safely down. A crag stands to the
south. Below, pick the best way through the bracken to find a path
falling to the road just before a wooden gate opening onto the lane.

TARN CRAG on SLEDDALE FELL, 2178FT/664M; HARROP PIKE, 2090FT/637M; GREY CRAG (LONGSLEDDALE), 2093FT/638M; GREAT HOWE (LONGSLEDDALE), 1621FT/494M

Maps: OS OL7, L90: GR 488078, GR 501078, GR 497072, GR 489064
Access point: Longsleddale, Sadgill Bridge, GR 483057
Distance/ascent: 6¼ mls/1770ft, 10km/540m
Approx time: 3½ hours

Follow the walled lane along the valley base to pass Buckbarrow Crag up to the right. As the track rises it becomes pitched with slate and begins to zigzag. Pass a gate to continue to the walls of a sheepfold. Bear right, signposted 'Mosedale', beneath the stone walls. Follow an indefinite path, that crosses and re-crosses the stream along Brownhowe Bottom. Rise to a gate on the col above the head of Mosedale. Bear right by the fence line to rise with the fence up the grassy north shoulder of Sleddale Fell. Stride the old fence which runs across and continue to a rise where the original line of fence turns a corner. Bear right to the rocky top of Tarn Crag standing above the masonry survey tower. Return to the fence and follow it into the hollow with the boggy ground of Greycrag Tarn (usually no tarn) on the right. Rise with the fence to its high corner. Bear left to follow it along the boggy shoulder towards Harrop Pike. Stride the fence, to follow its left side to the rocky knoll of Harrop Pike.

Return along the fence, bearing right (south) at its corner to follow a vague grassy path to the summit cairn of Grey Crag, located on a little bump higher than the rest. Head west to pick a way through the rocky outcrops and grass troughs. Descend to a built-in gap in the fence at its corner point. Pass through it and proceed along the spur of Great Howe. Another survey tower will be seen to the left before the highest rocky knoll of Great Howe is located. Again the path becomes indistinct and care must be exercised. Bear right, picking the best line down to a line of fence which, to the right becomes the fell wall. Cross the fence where it abuts the wall then bear right to find a natural corridor, leading down through the craggy ground. Thick bracken lies below but a path beats a way through it to a stile over the wall. Bear diagonally left across the field to a gate immediately above Sadgill Bridge.

28 KENTDALE GROUP

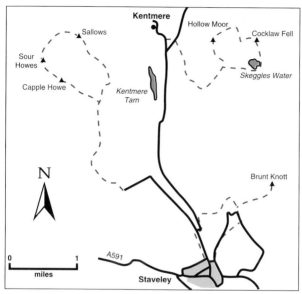

Location: Above the lower region of the River Kent, Eastern Fells.

Suggested Bases: Kendal, Kentdale and Windermere.

Accommodation: *Kendal:* all facilities; Kendal youth hostel; no camping. *Kentdale:* self-catering and b&b; several inns in Stavely; no youth hostel; camping at Rather Heath and Ashes Lane; bus service and train services between Kendal /Stavely/Windermere and from Stavely to Kentmere Village during the summer. *Windermere:* all facilities; youth hostel; camping at Park Cliffe and Tower Wood.

BRUNT KNOTT, 1400FT/427M

Maps: OS OL7, L90, L97: GR 484006

Access point: Stavely, above Barley Bridge, GR 470988

Distance/ascent: 5mls/1085ft, 8km/330m

Approx time: 2½ hours

Access Problems: Potter Fell and its three tops (including that of Ulgraves) have been excluded due to access problems.

 Proceed up the road beside the river to cross Scroggs Bridge. Continue to a small road, just before the hamlet of Fellside Cottages, climbing to the right towards Elf Howe. Bear right

on a lane between the houses of Middle Elfhowe and Lower
Elfhowe and ascend to the surfaced road of Hall Lane. A little way
along this a sign on the right points out a path which climbs the
field towards the farm of Ghyll Bank. Intercept a track beneath
the farm and bear right to a junction. Go left and ascend the road
to Brunt Knott Farm. Pass through the farm, through a gate and
over a stile. Follow the track which bears right up the fellside.
When the track divides, bear left to a grassy plateau. Bear left, up
the grassy flanks of Brunt Knott. The top of Brunt Howe is
marked by a stone trig point. Return through Brunt Knott Farm
bearing left at the junction and left again where the surfaced road
is joined. A signposted path bears down through the fields to the
right, to join Hall Lane. Descend the lane bearing right at the
bottom of the hill to cross Barley Bridge.

COCKLAW FELL, 1197FT/365M; HOLLOW MOOR on GREEN QUARTER FELL,
1398FT/426M

Maps: OS OL7, L90; GR 481039, GR 469040
Access point: Kentmere, limited parking, GR 456041
Distance/ascent: 6mls/1295ft, 8km/330m
Approx time: 3½ hours

From the church descend the road to cross Low Bridge and
turn left at the junction. In a short way a signposted path rises
through the field to the right. Above the buildings and the
surfaced Lowfield Lane, a track leads up to the right signposted
'Public Bridleway To Longsleddale via Cocklaw Fell'. Follow this,
taking the left fork at the junction. This grassy track ascends the
shoulder of Green Quarter Fell, with Skeggles Water now in sight.
Descend until just beyond the large ruined barn you join a further
track. Leave this and take the path right, across the low ground, to
traverse the southern edge of Skeggles Water. Take the wooden
footbridge across the exit stream to bear left across boggy ground.
A drainage ditch feeding the tarn is double-fenced and must be
crossed to the right. Proceed to the next inlet arm of the tarn and
stride the single fence where it meets the water. Take the rise
beyond and cross above the little crag and lonesome ash. Climb the
grassy flank of Cocklaw Fell. Bear left across a ruined wall and
ascend to the summit of Cocklaw Fell. Just to the north runs a wire
fence line (unmarked on OS maps). Cross it by climbing the sturdy
post at its corner point. Above lies the boggy and overgrown grassy
bridleway to Longsleddale. Bear left along it to a stile and gate
wall. Beyond this bear right through a wall gap to climb the grassy
shoulder above. Traverse left across a swampy hollow, then follow
the edge of the shoulder with an open view to the right. Stride a
fence line and ascend the grassy top of Hollow Moor on Green
Quarter Fell. Descend the flanks of the hill through rough pasture,
in the general direction of Skeggles Water to regain the grassy
bridleway (not obvious). Take the gate through the new fence and
the wall gap beyond, to return to the original junction of tracks by

the old barn. Bear right, making a slight ascent before the long
descent home.

CAPPLE HOWE, 1460FT/445M; SOUR HOWES, 1585FT/483M; SALLOWS,
1691FT/516M

Maps: OS OL7, L90: GR 432029, GR 428032, GR 433040
Access point: The end of Browfoot Lane above Kentmere provides
 limited parking, GR 448004
Distance/ascent: 6½ mls/1265ft, 10.5km/385m
Approx time: 3 hours

Take the walled track heading north. Keep right at the first
junction and continue to a gate. The track splits again. Take
the gate on the right and follow the track, with open ground to
the right and pasture over the wall to the left. Continue past a
walled enclosure and wood over to the right. Pass over a boggy
section and follow the track through a gate in the corner of the
wall to the right. Shortly, a circle of large rowans stand on the hill
above the track. A path bears left before these trees and crosses a
stream to round the corner of the fell wall. The path keeps right of
the wall, avoiding the bracken as best as possible, to find a gate at
the wall corner. This leads onto the open flanks of Capple Howe.
Bear right and make a strenuous ascent past the remains of stone
grouse butts en route to the grassy top of Capple Howe. Beyond, a
wall crosses the shoulder and behind it there's a triangular parcel
of fenced land. To its left, above the ruined wall a stile climbs the
fence. From here climb directly to the summit of Sour Howes. A
path falls through the grassy hillocks along the line of the wall to
the right. Rise to a wooden stile over a gated gap in the wall, take it
and proceed directly to the top of Sallows. There is a raised ridge
with a little cairn placed centrally, also known as Kentmere Park.
Proceed eastwards down the shoulder at first, to a stone shooting
butt. Bear right, falling directly down the flank of the hill to join
the old quarry track. Follow down this to enter a gated field. Walk
down this to the bridleway. Bear right exiting by a gate in the wall.
Park Beck flows directly in front. Bear left a little, before crossing
to find the track rising to the hill with the rowans.

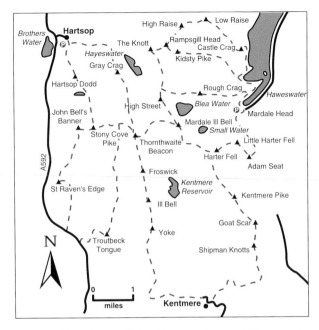

Location: Extending north from Kentmere between Ullswater and Haweswater, Eastern Fells.

Suggested Bases: Kendal, Kentdale, Windermere, Troutbeck, Ambleside, Ullswater, Lowther.

Accommodation: *Kendal:* all facilities; Kendal youth hostel; no camping. *Kentdale:* self-catering and b&b; several inns in Stavely; no youth hostel; camping at Rather Heath and Ashes Lane; bus service and train services between Kendal, Stavely and Windermere and from Stavely to Kentmere Village during the summer. *Windermere:* all facilities; youth hostel; camping at Park Cliffe and Tower Wood. *Troutbeck:* limited self-catering and b&b; Mortal Man and Queen's Head inns; Windermere youth hostel; camping at Limefitt Park. *Ambleside:* all facilities except railway station and campsite. Ambleside (Waterhead) youth hostel. *Ullswater:* self-catering and b&b; Brotherswater and Traveller's Rest inns; Patterdale and Helvellyn youth hostels; Swirral camping barn above Glenridding; camping at Sykeside by Brotherswater, Side Farm in Patterdale, various sites above Watermillock and east of the lake are to be found Park Foot, Hill Crest and

Waterside House; bus service from Penrith to Patterdale and Penrith to Keswick. *Lowther:* self-catering and b&b; several inns to be found in Askham, Helton, Shap and Bampton; no youth hostels, no bus service.

SHIPMAN KNOTTS, 1926FT/587M; GOAT SCAR, 2054FT/626M; KENTMERE PIKE, 2396FT/730M; HARTER FELL (MARDALE), 2552FT/778M; MARDALE ILL BELL, 2496FT/761M; THORNTHWAITE BEACON, 2572FT/784M; FROSWICK, 2360FT/720M; ILL BELL, 2483FT/757M; YOKE, 2316FT/706M

Maps: OS OL7, L90: GR 473063, GR 473069, GR 466078, GR 460093, GR 448101, GR 432100, GR 435085, GR 437077, GR 438067
Access point: Kentmere, limited parking, GR 456041
Distance/ascent: 12mls/3440ft, 19.5km/1040m
Approx time: 6¹/₂ hours

Take the walled lower lane below the church past Rook Howe Farm. Keep on the lane to dip around a bend to find (before a gate) a narrow stile gap in the wall on the right. A wooden footbridge crosses the young River Kent and a path rises to cross the walled track of Low Lane by two stiles. Climb the path directly to a stile leading onto the surfaced road of High Lane. Bear left, through a gate, to find a signed 'Public Bridleway to Sadgill & Longsleddale', unsurfaced track rising to the right. Follow this track, past the barns of Stile End to the left, until it begins to level where a grassy hillock and old quarry are to the left. Before the gate in the wall, lying at the highest point of this path, bear left to join the line of the wall and follow it steeply up the hillside. The angle eases, the wall turns a corner and the grassy bump of Wray Crag stands to the left. Keep with the path by the wall over a hollow of cotton grass before again making a steep ascent. The first knoll is cairned either side of the wall. It is the second knoll which constitutes the top of Shipman Knotts. Follow the path to a stile.

Above the stile follow the wire fence to the right to the top of Goat Scar – it is found within the corner of the fence. Follow the fence up the grassy shoulder of Kentmere Pike to its summit. The trig point stands just on the other side of the wall. Descend to Brown Howe then follow the fence directly up the shoulder to the large cairn on Harter Fell. The path to be followed bears west off the edge of the plateau. Descend to the head of Nan Bield Pass where the path rises, first to the left then swings back right. It levels along the shoulder before the path then splits. Bear right and make a steep ascent to the cairned top of Mardale Ill Bell. Bear left across the summit, leaving the path leading to High Street, to join with a lower path to the south. This path traverses the grassy hillside to intercept the broader route of the High Street Roman road. Bear right around the head of the hanging valley which holds Hayeswater, then climb up to the unmistakeable column of Thornthwaite Beacon. Descend the sweeping grassy shoulder and climb up to the first, the cairned top of Froswick. A descent and steep ascent gains Ill Bell. Proceed down the shoulder to the broader grassy summit of Yoke. The path leads down the shoulder to a stile over a stone wall. Cross this and follow the west side of the wall down to the head of the Garburn Pass and so back to Kentmere.

ST RAVEN'S EDGE, 1946FT/593M; JOHN BELL'S BANNER on CAUDALE MOOR, 2477FT/755M; STONY COVE PIKE, 2503FT/763M; TROUTBECK TONGUE, 1194FT/364M

Maps: OS OL7, L90: GR 403082, GR 413101, GR 418100, GR 423064
Access point: Small lay-by by the west side of the Kirkstone Pass A592 road, GR 412063
Distance/ascent: 7¹⁄₂ mls/2345ft, 12km/715m
Approx time: 4 hours

Proceed up the road to a gate and stile on the right. Follow the track into Woundale through a gate and cross an ancient stone-slab bridge. The path follows the wall to the right of the beck to rise steeply up the hillside to a large sheepfold. Bear left across the beck to climb grassy/boggy flanks to the track which leads to an old quarry. Ascend the hillside above to the crest of St Raven's Edge. A large cairn stands to the left and looks down to the Kirkstone Pass Inn. Cross the rocky knoll to the north, indicated on the OS as the highest point. The path continues by the wall into the dip. It then climbs up the long grassy flanks of John Bell's Banner. Follow the ruined wall line, over a rocky outcrop, until the path bears out left to a wooden cross in a cairn. This is Atkinson's Monument. Ascend beyond the cairn then bear left to the prominent cairn of John Bell's Banner which marks the top of Caudale Moor. Cross the moor past the tarn and return to the ruined wall. A little way along the wall cairns mark the highest top of Stony Cove Pike. Bear east along a path which traverses the rim of Park Fell Head, before joining the main trod by the stone wall. A steep descent leads to the col of Threshwaite Mouth. Bear right down a little path over a wide spread of stones. The path leads out onto a grassy tongue between two streams. Bear right to cross the small stream above the trees and continue along the path to a sheepfold. Cross Troutdale Beck at this point to walk above its east bank. Take a high contour to reach the gate in the stone wall, which encloses Troutdale Tongue. Beyond the gate you reach a sheepfold. Exit this by a further gate to the left. Follow the track for only a little way before bearing right to gain the grassy shoulder. Continue along the crest to stride a wire fence. Pass rocky knolls to the right to stand on the end bump of Troutdale Tongue. Double back for a short way until a route can be plotted to avoid the worst of the bracken down to the wire fence just above a large ash tree. Continue down the hillside skirting the northern edge of an alder wood, to an ancient stone-slab bridge. Cross the bridge and bear left along the west bank of Trout Beck. Above the confluence with Woundale Beck rise up the hillside to the right and follow a stone wall. At the field head cross the wall then cross Woundale Beck to the left to ascend a leaning stone wall. Climb the field above to a gate which exits directly onto Kirkstone Pass.

HARTSOP DODD, 2028FT/618M; STONY COVE PIKE, 2503FT/763M; GRAY CRAG, 2293FT/699M

Maps: OS OL5, L90: GR 412118, GR 418100, GR 427119
Access point: Hartsop, parking area through the hamlet
   GR 408132
Distance/ascent: 5¹/₂ mls/2755ft, 9km/840m
Approx time: 3¹/₂ hours

Take the kissing gate from the car park and immediately bear right, taking the bridge across Pasture Beck. Ascend the stony lane and walk through the gate/stile to bear right, up the steep grassy pasture by the stone wall. A narrow gate to the left leads through the fell wall. Bear right to ascend by the stone wall climbing the hillside. At the high corner of the wall the grassy path leads directly up the nose following a ruined wall to crest Hartsop Dodd. The path climbs the shoulder to the right of the stone wall. As the going levels, the cairn topping Stony Cove Pike is found to the left of the wall. A wall falls to Threshwaite Mouth and the main path follows this. The path rising to Threshwaite Beacon now lies above. Head north from the beacon cairn to the grassy path which descends to Gray Crag. Continue to the cairned nose end of the ridge. Although lower, this is hailed as the top of Gray Crag. The path falls steeply down the crest of the nose. About halfway down it steepens and becomes a little craggy. The path zigzags to avoid the worst and eventually joins the track which descends from Hayeswater to Hartsop.

HARTSOP DODD ABOVE ULLSWATER

ADAM SEAT, 2185FT/666M; LITTLE HARTER FELL, 2234FT/681M; HARTER
FELL (MARDALE), 2552FT/778M; MARDALE ILL BELL, 2496FT/761M; HIGH
STREET, 2718FT/828M; THE KNOTT (HIGH STREET), 2423FT/739M;
RAMPSGILL HEAD, 2598FT/792M; HIGH RAISE (HIGH STREET),
2633FT/802M; LOW RAISE, 2474FT/754M; CASTLE CRAG (MARDALE),
1296FT/395M

Maps: OS OL5, L90: GR 471091, GR 469095, GR 460093,
     GR 448101, GR 441111, GR 437127, GR 443128, GR 448134,
     GR 456137, GR 469127
Access point: Car park at Mardale Head at the head of
     Haweswater Reservoir, GR 469107
Distance/ascent: 10mls/3315ft, 16km/1010m
Approx time: 5¹/₂ hours

Follow the bridleway up Gatescarth Pass. At the col bear
right and follow the fence. At the corner stride the fence to the
top of Adam Seat. Return over the fence and follow it north
along the shoulder to intercept the main path. Above the path to
the right lies the rocky cairned top of Little Harter Fell. Beyond
this, climb the grassy shoulder of Harter Fell and round the corner
of the fence to a large cairn. Continue easily across the broad back
to the summit cairn of Harter Fell. Take the path which bears west
down the exposed edge between Mardale and Kentmere to the head
of Nan Bield Pass. Follow the path up to the shoulder, which falls
from Mardale Ill Bell. To reach the summit take the path bearing
right. A well-defined path cuts directly up the grassy shoulder of
High Street to intercept a stone wall. Follow the wall to the
concrete trig point of High Street. Descend following the wall.

The High Street Roman road enters from the left at the point
known as the Straits of Riggindale. Beyond the col keep to the path
which bears left. Follow along the stone wall to the top of The
Knott. Return to the path and cross it to climb directly up the
grassy flanks of Rampsgill Head. Intercept the main path and bear
left to a cairn. To the north near the cliffs stands a further cairn.
Between these two cairns lies the top. Take the path along the cliffs
and descend to a grassy col. A straightforward ascent leads to the
rock-strewn top of High Raise. Break from the main trod of the
High Street Roman road and take a lonely narrow path east to
Low Raise. Its top is marked by a substantial cairn and circular
stone shelter. Follow the south-east edge of Low Raise. Eventually
the edge steepens and a way must be picked through little craggy
outcrops down to Lady's Seat. To the left stands the independent
top of Castle Crag. Descent is probably best made to the north
where an ancient track becomes submerged in bracken. Descend to
the small enclosed wood before bearing right to the main path
which contours above Haweswater. Follow the path south.

ROUGH CRAG (RIGGINDALE), 2060FT/628M; HIGH STREET, 2718FT/828M;
RAMPSGILL HEAD, 2598FT/792M; KIDSTY PIKE, 2560FT/780M

Maps: OS OL5, L90: GR 454112, GR 441111, GR 443128,
     GR 448126
Access point: Car park at Mardale Head at the head of
     Haweswater Reservoir, GR 469107
Distance/ascent: 6¾ mls/2395ft, 11km/730m
Approx time: 3½ hours
Access problems: If the golden eagles are nesting (April-July), this
     walk may be deemed out of bounds by the RSPB.

Take the kissing gate, cross the bridge and then bear right.
Bear right again to cross the bridge over Mardale Beck,
rounding the head of Haweswater. Continue to rise above the
sweet-smelling conifer woods which now occupy The Rigg. Bear left
up the path skirting the bracken along the toe of the ridge. Follow
the steepening path up the increasingly rocky ridge on the left side
of the wall to crest the cairned top of Rough Crag. Descend to the
col and tarn of Caspel Gate. Make a steep ascent up Long Stile to
emerge suddenly by the cairn on the edge of the flat grassy plateau
of High Street. The summit trig point lies a little way over to the
left. Follow the path over the hump of Short Stile to the right,
before reaching the col and Straits Of Riggindale.
     Take the path which rises to the right over Twopenny Crag
with an open view into empty Riggindale below. Bear left to the
cairns of Rampsgill Head before returning right to the obvious
upturned nose of Kidsty Crag. A path bears easily down the grassy
shoulder to find a natural corridor leading safely through the crags
of Kidsty Howes. Descend the grassy flanks below to join the main
valley path just beyond the stone-arched bridge over Randale
Beck. Bear right along the path and cross the footbridge over
Riggindale Beck. Climb the rocky steps to pass through the corner
of a larch wood. The path now bears out rightwards from the
ancient aisle, to climb the fields and round The Rigg.

30 MARTINDALE GROUP

Location: East of Ullswater between Patterdale and Howtown, Eastern Fells.

Suggested Base: Ullswater.

Accommodation: *Ullswater:* self-catering and b&b; Brotherswater and Traveller's Rest inns; Patterdale and Helvellyn youth hostels; Swirral camping barn above Glenridding; camping at Sykeside by Brotherswater, Side Farm in Patterdale, various sites above Watermillock and east of the lake are to be found Park Foot, Hill Crest and Waterside House; bus service from Penrith to Patterdale and Penrith to Keswick.

LOW BIRK FELL, 1224FT/373M; BLEABERRY KNOTT on BIRK FELL, 1680FT/512M; THE KNIGHT, 1778FT/542M; PLACE FELL, 2154FT/657M; HIGH DODD, 1644FT/501M; SLEET FELL, 1240FT/378M

Maps: OS OL5, L90: GR 411190, GR 403183, GR 404176, GR 406170, GR 416182, GR 423189

Access point: Sandwick, limited parking by the end of the surfaced road, GR 423196

Distance/ascent: 5mls/2425ft, 8km/740m
Approx time: 3¹/₂ hours

 Leave Sandwick by the track signposted 'Patterdale'. Follow above the stone wall to an old stone barn on the right. Shortly after this bear right to a footbridge across Scalehow Beck. Rise with the track until at its highest point, above the corner in the wall, a path rises directly up the open fellside to the right. Scalehow Force is visible to the left, through the trees. The path bears left slightly until the angle eases on a slight shoulder. It now zags to the right above the little rocky craglets to the nose of the fell. Ascend this directly to the top of Low Birk Fell. Descend along the path through the brackeny hollows with rocky bumps to the right. Proceed across the hollow to the rim, with a view above Ullswater. Bear left over the bracken of Kilbert How to find a rising diagonal path across the steep flanks above. Follow the path for some 20m then climb directly up the steep hillside to a cairned bilberry-clad top above Smeathwaite.

Proceed across the heather and bilberry shoulder to the dome of Bleaberry Knott which is the summit of Birk Fell. In front lies the Matterhorn-like The Knight. Place Fell is visible beyond. Skirt the low boggy ground to the right to cross an area of whaleback rocky knolls and grassy boggy hollows. Suddenly appearing beyond the undulations a well-defined path rises from Ullswater and climbs the grassy flanks above. At a col bear left along the narrow grassy rocky ridge to find the summit of The Knight. Return to the path at the col and continue the ascent, over a subsidiary ridge to the summit of Place Fell. The trig point lies on the rocky spur just to the east. A good path leaves the summit rocks to pass a little tarn in a hollow and heads north-east along the shoulder of Hart Crag. The path leads on to the col of Low Moss. Beyond the sheepfold the path divides.

Take the right fork, rising to a shoulder on the flank of High Dodd. At this point, as the path levels before descending, bear left to climb directly to the summit of High Dodd. The best descent is found to the right down the grassy eastern flank. Descend through the bracken to gain the main path. Follow this and bear left along the shoulder. The path leads to the grassy top of Sleet Fell. Continue to the last grassy rise. In front there's an old ruined wall and over this a large cairn. The most straightforward descent is to follow the line of the wall down the western flank of the fell. Near the bottom the wall disappears into thick bracken. A path prevails, bearing slightly left before falling to a track (which has descended from the col of Low Moss). Continue directly back to Sandwick.

BEDA HEAD on BEDA FELL, 1670FT/509M; ANGLETARN PIKE NORTH, 1860FT/567M; ANGLETARN PIKE SOUTH, 1854FT/565M; BROCK CRAGS, 1842FT/561M; REST DODD, 2283FT/696M; THE NAB, 1890FT/576M

Maps: OS OL5, L90: GR 417137, GR 413148, GR 414147,
GR 417137, GR 433137, GR 434152

Access point: Martindale, parking below the Old Church of St
    Martin, GR 434183
Distance/ascent: 8³/₄ mls/2740ft, 14km/835m
Approx time: 5 hours
Access problems: At the time of writing landowner/tenant
    Mr Hasell-McCosh of Dalemain Estates, Penrith has objected
    to the use of the path over The Nab: route described by
    A.Wainwright, *The Far Eastern Fells*, 1957.

Cross Christy Bridge and pass the farm buildings which stand
to the right. Take the path rising to the right. Cross a track
and ascend the hillside by the wall. When the track crests the
brow, bear left along it over the rocky turrets of Winter Crag.
Beyond, a grassy ascent up the nose of Beda Fell, passes an ancient
cairn on a rocky knoll to the right, before gaining the grassy top of
Beda Head. A small cairn stands on a knoll of rock. A well-defined
path continues along the ridge, first falling then rising again to the
cairned shoulder of Bedafell Knott. Beyond this the ridge is crossed
by an ancient packhorse route rising from Boredale Hause and
falling to Dale Head. Continue along the ridge past a cairn on a
knoll, until the path levels to cross an area of grassy hummocks
above Heckbeck Head. Bear right off the path to the highest grassy
dome. Head straight for the rocky tower of Angletarn Pike North.
Leave it and cross the grassy divide to scramble easily to the top of
the second pike, Angletarn Pike South.

    Pick the easiest line of descent and weave a way through
the craggy ground below. Cross two paths and descend to the
hollow by the tarn. Stride the little stream from the tarn, and pass
through a gap in the stone wall to ascend Cat Crags. Cross a
further wall gap before bearing right, by an old structure of flat
slabby stones, to the summit cairn of Brock Crags. Leave the
summit, following the path over boggy ground to the left of a little
tarn. Follow the line of an old stone wall to a junction with the
path rising from Angle Tarn. Take the gate on the right and
continue along the well-trod path. Satura Crag lies unseen below to
the left. Bear right when the path appears to diverge. The path
continues along the line of a fence. It bears right at a point where
the line of an old wall sweeps directly up the grassy flanks of Rest
Dodd. At the end of the line of the old wall bear left to the summit
cairn of Rest Dodd. Descend the steep northern nose of this to find
a stone wall which crosses its flanks. This is the barrier of the deer
park. The gap that existed allowing access has been filled and no
gate/stile inserted in its place.

    Those wishing to continue along this long-established route to
one of The Lake National Park's separate fell tops will now have to
surmount the wall. Cross and follow the path down and across the
shoulder to rise up the broad grassy head of The Nab. Head south-
west to find an old stalkers track. This turns to traverse the steep
western flank of The Nab, passing beneath Nab End, before
descending the lower section of the nose. A gate leads through the
wall and the path/track continues directly down the easier
shoulder below. Bear right at the next stone wall to find a gate.

Take this and cross to the unsurfaced track beyond. Bear left to gain the road and follow this down Martindale. The track is also private and provides access to 'The Bungalow', now a holiday home advertised by Dalemain Estates. An alternative finish to this walk could be to extend it onto High Street Roman Road before making descent by Gowk Hill as described next.

GOWK HILL, 1545FT/471M; BROWNTHWAITE CRAG, 1457FT/444M; PIKEAWASSA on STEEL KNOTTS, 1417FT/432M; HALLIN FELL, 1273FT/388M

Maps: OS OL5, L90: GR 445167, GR 443174, GR 440181, GR 433198
Access point: Martindale, lay-by opposite St Peter's Church, GR 436191
Distance/ascent: 5mls/1725ft, 8km/525m
Approx time: 2³/₄ hours

Pass the church gate to gain the open fellside by Lanty Tarn. Bear right to make a high traverse beneath the craggy lower face of Birkie Knot, to follow above the stone wall. When open ground falls away to the right to the Old Church of St Martin, descend to intercept a path which rises from the surfaced road. Follow the path, above the fell wall, to take the gap (the highest one) in the wall which forms the boundary of Martindale Forest. The path rises to cross a bank of slate and passes the opening marked on the OS map as 'Cave', continuing to traverse the hillside. Pass above the next wooded area and cross a small gill. Before reaching Mell Beck, at a point where 'The Bungalow' is in sight below, the path disappears. Ascend the grassy flanks to the grassy dome of Gowk Hill. A few stones stand on its western edge. The top will be found across a hollow of marshy ground to the east.

Now begins the traverse of the edge, with Martindale below to the west and Fusedale to the east. Bear right down the grassy flanks to meet a well-defined path. Follow the path until it splits. Take the right fork which climbs to the grassy summit of Brownthwaite Crag. Following the line of the wall, make a descent down a groove in the crag. Continue in the same line to eventually cross the wall (gap), where it turns to cross the edge. Make a steep ascent to the turreted Pikeawassa. Proceed along Steel Knotts until, at the highest cairned top above the descent to Steel End, a path bears off to the left. Follow the path which zigzags down the shoulder past the two tiered crags of Birkie Knott, before descending to Lanty Tarn. Cross the road and pass your starting point.

Take the main grassy drag straight up the flanks of Hallin Fell. On the shoulder overlooking Ullswater bear right to reach the 12ft-high cairn which marks the summit. Follow the path descending eastwards, looking directly over Ullswater's last leg towards Pooley Bridge. Continue down, through a natural cleft past little craggy outcrops until a distinct path bears off to the right.

31 CONISTON MASSIF

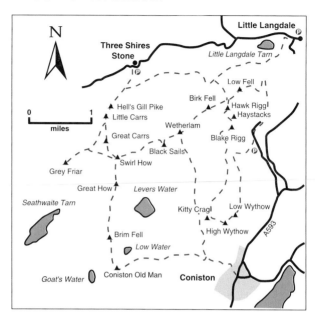

Location: North of Coniston, south of the Wrynose Pass/Little
Langdale road, Southern Fells.

Suggested Bases: Coniston and Little Langdale.

Accommodation: *Coniston:* self-catering and b&b; limited
facilities; Holly How and Coppermines House youth hostels;
camping at Coniston Hall. *Little Langdale:* limited self-
catering and b&b at The Three Shires Inn.

HELL GILL PIKE, 2172FT/662M; LITTLE CARRS, 2270FT/692M; GREAT CARRS,
2575FT/785M; SWIRL HOW, 2630FT/802M; GREY FRIAR, 2536FT/773M

Maps: OS OL6, L90: GR 269016, GR 270015, GR 270009,
GR 273005, GR 260004

Access point: The Three Shires Stone at the summit of Wrynose
Pass, GR 277027

Distance/ascent: 4¹/₂ mls/1740ft, 7.5km/530m

Approx time: 3 hours

A path rises to the south of the road, just beyond the summit
rocks of the pass. Although initially steep, it levels to contour
the hillside before steepening suddenly and zigzagging back left

to climb to a little cairn on Wet Side Edge. The edge is no more than a steady climb. As it gains an easier shoulder, an independent rock island to the right of the path offers a cairned top, Hell Gill Pike. The path rises to a rocky niche through the crest of the shoulder. To the left a rocky protuberance marks the top of Little Carrs. A flat area and a lower hollow separates Little Carrs from Great Carrs above. Take the path which weaves up the rocky turret to the left (the path leaving the hollow to the right traverses over Wether How in the direction of Grey Friar and will be used in descent). Pass the head of a further gully and walk easily up a slope to the outcrop of white rhyolite crowned by a cairn – the summit of Great Carrs. Follow the shoulder on its Greenburn edge to the curved stony-rimmed col known as the Top Of Broad Slack passing on the right the remains of an aircraft.

The climb levels towards the summit of Swirl How. Briefly retrace your steps to the col. Make straight west down easy slopes to the meeting of paths on the grassy pastures of Fairfield. Then walk to the stony top of Grey Friar. Two cairned rock outcrops adorn the summit area. The most south-easterly is the higher. Return to Fairfield and take the path which leads off to the left (north). It leads easily over Wether How to rejoin the original path in the hollow beneath the top of Little Carrs.

BIRK FELL MAN on BIRK FELL, 1722FT/525M; WETHERLAM, 2502FT/762M; BLACK SAILS, 2443FT/745M; SWIRL HOW, 2630FT/802M; GREAT CARRS, 2575FT/785M; LITTLE CARRS, 2270FT/692M

Maps: OS OL6, L90: GR 296017, GR 288011, GR 283008, GR 273005, GR 270009, GR 270015
Access point: Little Langdale village, GR 316033
Distance/ascent: 8³/₄ mls/3200ft, 14km/975m
Approx time: 5¹/₂ hours

Take road to crossroads at the top of the hill. Turn left down the drive to High Birk How Farm, before which the gate on the right leads across fields down to Slaters Bridge. Cross the bridge and the field beyond to a walled track and turn right. Follow the track passing Low and High Hall Garth, go through a gate and cross a little stream. The track rises then levels. Ignore a track which forks back up to the left. Just past the head of the tarn, the track to Greenburn branches off left. Follow the track to a stone wall. Cross the stile by the gate then bear left to follow the wall up the fellside. As the going levels near the head of Birk Fell Gill a rocky knoll rises to the right. Circumnavigate this and rise to a post and wire fence. Bear right past a stile then go round the corner of the fence. Take the second stile to gain the flanks of Birk Fell. Climb the hillside, first moving to the left and then climb more directly picking the easiest way to the top of Birk Fell, Birk Fell Man. There are two cairns on two different rock outcrops, both seem of equal altitude. Continue along the shoulder of Birkfell Hause to climb Wetherlam Edge. The going levels and the summit cairn on a rocky outcrop is reached.

The path traverses the northern flanks of the mountain. Beneath the head of Black Sail make a direct, virtually pathless ascent. Descend to regain the main trod and follow it down into the col of Swirl Hawse. In front Prison Band climbs to the top of Swirl How. Descend to the broad rimmed col – Top Of Broad Slack. Continue to the cairned rock outcrop on the edge of the precipice which marks the summit of Great Carrs. The path leads down the rim to a hollow. The top of Little Carrs is just to the right. Either follow the edge, with views down into Greenburn or move right to the main path. Both ways lead over a broad shoulder to Wet Side Edge. Plunge rapidly down the edge, until slowed by the steeper and rockier end of the edge known as Rough Crags. The path bears down to the right and is straightforward. Beneath the steepest section, follow the broad shoulder until the path forks off down to the right to a stone wall falling to Greenburn Beck. Crossing the beck shouldn't prove too difficult. Just above lies the main track back to Little Langdale.

GREAT INTAKE on LOW FELL, 1327FT/405M; HIGH FELL, 1404FT/428M; HAWK RIGG, 1447FT/441M; HAYSTACKS (TILBERTHWAITE), 1381FT/421M; BLAKE RIGG (TILBERTHWAITE), 1388FT/423M; KITTY CRAG, 1427FT/435M; LONG CRAG on YEWDALE FELLS, 1381FT/421M; HIGH WYTHOW, 1345FT/410M; LOW WYTHOW, 1220FT/372M; BRACKENY CRAG, 1212FT/370M

Maps: OS OL6, L90: GR 303022, GR 300017, GR 300015, GR 301014, GR 301012, GR 295990, GR 298990, GR 300990, GR 303993, GR 303998

Access point: Tilberthwaite car park, GR 306010

Distance/ascent: 6¼ mls/1805ft, 10km/550m

Approx time: 3¾ hours

Cross the bridge and proceed to High Tilberthwaite Farm. Take the high gate on the left out of the farmyard and follow a rough track, passing through a gate to gain the highest point of the track. Just beyond, a grassy track loops off to the left rising gently to a gate and stile in a stone wall.

Take the stile then follow the track to the right passing an open level on the left. It climbs the toe of the quarry bank and passes a ruined building on the right. To the left quarry works have created a narrow rift running up the hillside. Initially keep to the right to round a bank of slate spoil, then cross a low stone wall. Climb the right edge of the rift until it is easier to traverse right into a rough stream bed. Move up its right bank. Climb to reach a boggy area with another slate spoil heap over to the left. Circumnavigate the bog to the right then climb rough heathery ground. Cross rightwards towards the elevated massif of Great Intake and climb its steep flanks at the midway point. Up to the left lies the final rocky knoll of Great Intake. To climb it, first bear slightly left on a sheep trod. Make an awkward rocky step in an exposed position before easier climbing gains the summit cairn.

Descend first right then left taking care to avoid two craggy outcrops. A hollow boggy area leads to a stile over the stone wall. Walk round the rocky knoll, then take the first stile over the wire fence. Climb directly, passing twisted and gnarled stunted larch trees, to reach the summit and cairn of High Fell. Descend into the dip beyond and pass through a crown of larch to gain the open head of Hawk Rigg. The summit lies beyond a little tarn. Descend steeply through thick larch. Move slightly left, taking care to avoid the steepest craggy section. Initially follow a corridor below the grassy hump of Haystacks then climb to its summit. Head straight down towards Blake Rigg. Rise gently up its shoulder to the final rock outcrops which mark the summit. Return down the shoulder of Blake Rigg until it is possible to head due west across the peat moss to pick up a track rising up the edge of Dry Cove Bottom.

Descend the track until a sweeping bend brings the head of the distant Tilberthwaite Gill into sight. Bear right above some old mine buildings passing a deep unprotected rift (the fence is ruined -- keep away as this hole is very dangerous). Cross the beck just below a pleasant rocky cascade. Bear first left, keeping high above the moss to find the high miners' track which circumnavigates Yewdale Moss. The track eventually crosses beneath mine workings to a further track. Continue along this to cross a stream. Bear slightly right and ascend the slope to regain the track. Follow this past Hole Tarn on the right. At the highest point of the track bear up the grassy flanks to the left. Traverse left to the cairned top of Kitty Crag. Cross the hollow, ascend a grassed-over track to the long edge of Long Crag. A dished shield of rock adorns the top. Pass a little tarn on the right and ascend High Wythow. The grassy hump is Low Wythow. Head due north. There is no real path but with care an easy route can be selected which weaves through the rocky knolls and bracken to Brackeny Crag. Yewdale Moss lies to the east. Descend first north, then west to a distinct grassed track through a natural corridor. Move west, leaving this track behind, to pick up a well-worn path which circumnavigates the moss on its eastern edge. Follow this until it dips and crosses Crook Beck. Rise to the right along a smaller path which leads down the south bank (true right) of Tilberthwaite Gill.

OLD MAN of CONISTON, 2633FT/803M; BRIM FELL, 2611FT/796M; GREAT HOW on SWIRL BAND, 2526FT/770M; SWIRL HOW, 2630FT/802M; BLACK SAILS, 2443FT/745M; WETHERLAM, 2502FT/762M

Maps: OS OL6, L90: GR 273978, GR 271986, GR 273000, GR 273005, GR 283008, GR 288011
Access point: Coniston village, GR 300979
Distance/ascent: 7³/₄ mls/3150ft, 12.5km/960m
Approx time: 5 hours

Take the road rising to the Coppermines Valley. Easy walking leads to the Miners Bridge across Church Beck. A well-worn path skirts the south side of the beck for a way until, after a

WETHERLAM

stile, it begins to rise to the left. On Crowberry Hows the path
joins with the quarry tracks which lead easily to Low Water. It
then rises again until a final section of path leads to the summit
cairn of the Old Man of Coniston. A gentle descent and ascent
leads north along the shoulder to the curved top of Brim Fell.
Descend again to Levers Hause, rise to the protuberance of Great
How and up Swirl Band to the circular beehive cairn which marks
the summit of Swirl How. Descend Prison Band to the right. The
path rises to skirt Black Sails and then on to Wetherlam. A route
leads along on an easy shoulder above large cliffs to descend the
ridge of Lad Stones. At the track go right and descend into the
Coppermines Valley.

32 DOW CRAG GROUP

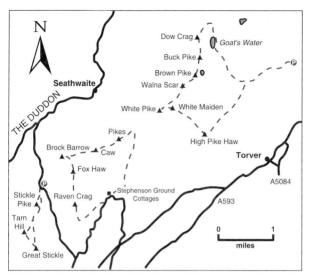

N

Dow Crag ▲
Goat's Water
Buck Pike ▲
Brown Pike ▲ **0**
Seathwaite
Walna Scar ▲
THE DUDDON
White Pike ▲ ← White Maiden
Pikes
Brock Barrow ▲ Caw
High Pike Haw ▲
▲ Fox Haw
Torver
Stickle Pike ▲
Raven Crag ▲ ■ Stephenson Ground Cottages
A5084
Tarn Hill
A593
Great Stickle

0　　　　　1
miles

Location: South of The Duddon and north of Coniston Water, Southern Fells.

Suggested Bases: Coniston, Broughton in Furness and The Duddon.

Accommodation: Coniston: self-catering and b&b; limited facilities; Holly How and Coppermines House youth hostels; camping at Coniston Hall. *Broughton:* limited facilities; no youth hostel; no camping. *The Duddon:* self-catering and b&b; The Newfield Inn at Seathwaite; The Blacksmith's Arms at Broughton Mills; no youth hostel; camping at Turner Hall.

DOW CRAG, 2554FT/778M; BUCK PIKE on SEATHWAITE FELL, 241FT/744M; BROWN PIKE, 2237FT/682M; WALNA SCAR, 2037FT/621M; WHITE PIKE (SEATHWAITE), 1962FT/598M; WHITE MAIDEN, 1995FT/608M; HIGH PIKE HAW, 1161FT/354M

Maps: OS OL6, L96: GR 263978, GR 262972, GR 261966, GR 258963, GR 249956, GR 254957, GR 264949

Access point: The Walna Scar road above Coniston, GR 289970

Distance/ascent: 7³/₄ mls/2280ft, 12.5km/695m

Approx time: 4¹/₂ hours

Proceed along the track until it begins to zigzag steeply up the face of Old Man of Coniston to Brossan Stones Quarry (named Bursting Stones on the map). The Walna Scar road breaks off to

the left. Follow it past tiny Boo Tarn until a path breaks off right, beside a small cairn, to rise steeply up a grassy bank. The path joins a rough track and levels to cross The Cove. It sweeps around Goat's Crag and rises to a fine view over Goatswater to Dow Crag. Continue along the eastern shore of Goat's Water to climb steeply to the col of Goat's Hawse. Bear left to scramble up the final rock outcrop of Dow Crag. A stony path along a ruined wall leads along the high shoulder to Buck Pike. Continue to the summit of Brown Pike. An easy descent leads across the col which marks the summit of the Walna Scar road. A slight ascent leads to the top of Walna Scar, a long grassy shoulder broken only by the flaggy outcrops of slate.

Continue along the shoulder and bear right under White Maiden to the top of White Pike. Head for the rocky top of White Maiden then descend the shoulder to the left of the wall. There is no path but the going is straightforward until the top of Dropping Crag is reached. With a little care a descent route can be selected to enter a secluded little valley beneath. The shoulder continues to the knobbly dome of High Pike Haw. From its rocks take a high route skirting the bog of High Torver Common. Cross Ash Gill Beck and follow it past the deep hole of an old slate working. Above the wall, a path leads over Torver Beck and makes a steep ascent to the Walna Scar road.

PIKES, 1539FT/469M; CAW, 1735FT/529M; BROCK BARROW, 1125FT/343M; FOX HAW, 1263FT/385M; RAVEN'S CRAG, 1184FT/361M

Maps: OS OL6, L96: GR 238947, GR 230945, GR 220943, GR 223936, GR 224929
Access point: Opposite Stephenson Ground Cottages (very limited), GR 235931
Distance/ascent: 5¼ mls/1675ft, 8.5km/510m
Approx time: 3¼ hours

From the cottages follow the road between the old stone barns of Stephenson Ground. A gate on the left, signposted 'Bridleway Walna Scar', leads to an open track which continues along the stone wall through a little gate to traverse open fellside. Pass beneath a little crag through a gap in the wall. After a gill falls over a craggy outcrop to the left, the track begins to rise. To the right, at the end of the trees, the main beck bears off to cut a deep ravine. Our track rises to the left before it crosses a stream, to join a crossroads. Take the track rising to the left. Where the path levels, Dawson Pike is seen ahead with two patches of vivid white quartz. Cross the stream to the left and climb to the left to find a notch in the first rocky bump. A slight sheep trod can be followed for most of the way. Pass a hollow and a marshy tarn, before making an ascent to the three rocky outcrops which mark the summit of Pikes.

Ahead lies Caw. Descend and follow a slight sheep trod which eventually makes a steep winding ascent to gain the the trig point of Caw. Descend to the right following a faint path in the direction of the distant head of Long Mire. This path finds a narrow, steep but easy rock-filled gully through the cliff of Goat Crag. This leads

safely down to the head of Long Mire. Bear right to join the track
and left to cross the stream. Follow the track to its high point then
hop the stone wall on the right. Traverse right to an easy ascent
through the crag of slatey blocks. This leads to a second rocky
outcrop, which is the summit of Brock Barrow. An easy ascent can
be made from the west. Reverse the ascent to regain the track and
find a vague track which rises from it. The ridge beyond runs
along the length of Dunnerdale, comprising many rocky outcrops
and grassy bumps. The track rises around the first rocky bump to
the left. Pass through further knolls to regain the path. Continue
to the obviously larger summit rise of Fox Haw. A short squat
cairn has been skillfully constructed over the sharp-edged summit
ridge. Descend then ascend directly to the next slatey hill.

Descend again then make for the cairn on the first and highest
top of Raven's Crag. Beyond, a little valley-like hollow leads along
the crest to the next lower top which is the last high bump of the
shoulder. A path breaks off left and descends to a col crossed by a
distinct track. Bear left along the track. The track crosses Black
Moss Beck before rising to the left, slightly away from the wall.
Pass the buildings of Jackson Ground to a metal gate, before a
barn of modern construction. Walk through the farmyard and
down the lane to the surfaced road.

STICKLE PIKE, 1231FT/375M; TARN HILL, 1027FT/313M; GREAT STICKLE,
1001FT/305M

Maps: OS OL6, L96 GR 212928, GR 210921, GR 2129176
Access point: Kiln Bank Cross, GR 214933
Distance/ascent: 2¹/₂ mls/705ft, 4km/215m
Approx time: 1¹/₂ hours

An ancient grassed track rises from Kiln Bank. Cross past the
northern end of Stickle Tarn. Above the tarn leave the track
and make a climb directly for the summit. Slightly beneath
and to the west of the southern end of Stickle Pike, a grassy
corridor leads down through the steep rocky flanks. Some slatey
scree at the bottom leads to a good track (the continuation of the
original). This falls through thick bracken to the hollow below.
Cross the top of the bog, rise over a slight shoulder, then fall again
into a slight corridor. To the right, the track continues to the
summit area of the perfectly named Tarn Hill. Descent leads to a
grassy plateau beneath Great Stickle. Ascend the flank of the hill
to the summit and trig point. A path bears diagonally down across
the flank of Great Stickle. Pass under some small crags and a
ruined stone structure to gain the moss which feeds Red Moss
Beck. Circumnavigate the bog, then return to the original track
and follow this until it begins to rise up the eastern flank of Stickle
Pike. Bear right beneath a rock bluff, with a holly growing in its
centre and a ruined building beneath it. Rise and cross the small
stream of Hare Hall Beck en route for Stickle Tarn.

33 HARTER FELL GROUP

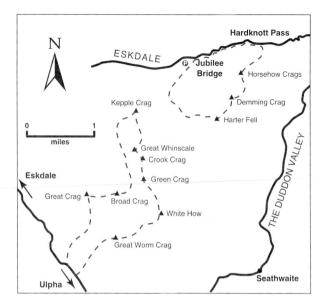

Location: A triangle of fells between Eskdale, The Duddon and the
Birker Moor Road, Southern Fells.

Suggested Bases: The Duddon and Eskdale.

Accommodation: The Duddon: self-catering and b&b; The
Newfield Inn at Seathwaite; The Blacksmith's Arms at
Broughton Mills; no youth hostel; camping at Turner Hall.
Eskdale: self-catering accomodation and b&b at The
Burnmoor and The Woolpack Inns; Eskdale youth hostel;
camping at Boot, Fisherground Farm.

HARTER FELL (ESKDALE), 2141FT/653M; DEMMING CRAG, 1722FT/525M;
HORSEHOW CRAGS, 1421FT/433M

Maps: OS OL6, L90, L96: GR 219997, GR 222002, GR 224008
Access point: Foot of Hardknott Pass just above the cattle grid,
GR 213011
Distance/ascent: 4¹/₂ mls/1970ft, 7.5km/600m
Approx time: 3¹/₂ hours

 Hardknott Gill is crossed by Jubilee Bridge, below the road.
Climb the steps to find a good track crossing the flanks of the
fell. Two kissing gates lead to the open track of solid construction.

BIRKER FELL

Follow it to cross Dodknott Gill and walk through a gate in the stone
wall. The track passes through another gate and climbs the open
fellside. At a cairn on the left the path bears off to ascend Harter
Fell. Take it through thick bracken then up the open heather-clad
hillside. The path climbs to the right of some crags to the summit of
Harter Fell. Turn left up to the trig point situated on the most
southerly of the three summit outcrops. The next rock outcrop, the
middle one, is the highest. A path leads north in the direction of
Hardknott Pass. Some way down, the domed top of Demming Crag
stands to the left. Traverse left and ascend to the grass and rock top.
Descend the same way and bear down the left bank of the small ravine
of Castlehow Beck. Walk over the remains of a ruined wall to regain
the main path where it crosses the gill. Leave the main path
immediately and sweep back left to a great bog beneath the craggy
face of Demming Crag. Skirt it on the right until a crossing can be
made to a stile below a gate over the wire fence. There is no real path
here, only rough grass and bog. Rise leftwards to the rocky top of
Horsehow Crags (the outcrop to the left, nearest the edge feels
highest). Make a boggy trudge back right to find the main path above
the forestry fence. The path leads round into a hollow with a pond on
the left. A stile climbs a fence, then a track bears left down onto the
Hardknott Pass.

GREAT WORM CRAG, 1400FT/427M; WHITE HOW on BIRKER FELL, 1457FT/
444M; GREEN CRAG, 1604FT/489M; CROOK CRAG, 1539FT/469M; GREAT
WHINSCALE, 1394FT/425M; KEPPLE CRAG, 1076FT/328M; BROAD CRAG on
BIRKER FELL, 1220FT/372M; GREAT CRAG on BIRKER FELL, 1109M/338M

Maps: OS OL6, L96 GR 194969, GR 205975, GR 200983,
GR 200988, GR 198990, GR 199999, GR 195978, GR 186978

Access point: Birker Moor, beyond Winds Gate cattle grid,
   GR 184958
Distance/ascent: 7¹/₂ mls/1690ft, 12km/515m
Approx time: 4 hours

From the road a footpath leads up the true right bank of
Freeze Beck and bears left over a short boggy section. The
path rises to skirt the eastern flanks of Rough Crag. An easy
ascent leads over rough fell grass to a large circular pile of stones.
Continue directly ahead to climb the final grassy dome of Great
Worm Crag. Dipping slightly, proceed along the pathless shoulder
towards White How. A swing left gives access to the rocky dome of
Far Hill; the highest point marked by a cairn. At the lowest point of
the shoulder, cross a narrow boggy section. Ascend and bear left
around a little crag to the rocky summit of White How. Walk down
to the col, which is a little boggy, then ascend along the easiest line
towards Green Crag. A rocky knoll, a dip and another rise lead to a
further rocky turret with a curious black overhanging slab to the
right. Left of this an easy grass rake leads up and over a worn
slabby block. A steep ascent to the right leads to a rock outcrop
and cairn. The final tower of Green Crag rises beyond. A path
swings up the right then back left to the rocky summit.

Descend due north in the direction of Crook Crag. Soon the
path veers right along a natural grass shelf before descending to
the grassy col below. Past the col to the left stands The Pike, a
conical protuberance ringed by scree. A path continues beneath
the end of Crook Crag. Bear right, contour round to a short rock
groove and scramble up this. A few easy rocky steps lead to the
top. Its summit cairn stand on the western end of an elongated
rock ridge. Descend the same way and continue along the path
with a large balanced block to the right. Shortly afterwards it is
worth climbing up to the top of Great Whinscale. Return to the
path by the same route. After descending slightly bear right over
thick heather and bilberry, aiming for a natural corridor between
two rock outcrops. Pass a crag on the left and rise to the rocky
summit of Kepple Crag. From the western edge of the summit a
way down can be seen to the left. Descend with caution to the
heather and bracken beneath the crag.

Continue leftwards to a level platform in the slope of the
hillside. Pass a small ruined enclosure and rise to a notch in the
shoulder. Contour the hillside to the rocky ridge of Great
Whinscale standing above to the left. Rise slightly onto the
shoulder of the ridge. Continue to contour the hillside, dropping
only slightly to a boggy area and cairned path rising from below.
Skirt above the bogs until you're below Green Crag. Splodge across
to the topmost rocky knoll of Broad Crag. Continue easily down
the grassy shoulder of Meeting Hill and cross the tiny Rowantree
Beck. Cross the low ruined perimeter wall around Great Crag. The
distinctive cairned middle finger appears to be the highest point.
Return to cross the ruined wall and strike a contour back over
Highfold Beck. Stay as high as possible before skirting beneath
Rough Crag to a shoulder. It leads back to the road.

34 WHITFELL GROUP

Location: Western fringe south of Eskdale and north of the
 Corney Fell Road, Southern Fells.
Suggested Bases: The Duddon and Eskdale.
Accommodation: The Duddon: self-catering and b&b; The
 Newfield Inn at Seathwaite; The Blacksmith's Arms at
 Broughton Mills; no youth hostel; camping at Turner Hall.
 Eskdale: self-catering accomodation and b&b at The
 Burnmoor and The Woolpack Inns; Eskdale youth hostel;
 camping at Boot, Fisherground Farm.

ROUGH CRAG (BIRKER MOOR), 1047FT/319M; WATER CRAG,
1001FT/305M; THE KNOTT on STAINTON FELL, 1086FT/331M; WHITE PIKE
on BIRKBY FELL, 1450FT/442M; WOODEND HEIGHT, 1597FT/487M;
YOADCASTLE, 1621FT/494M; SEAT HOW (BIRKER MOOR), 1020FT/311M

Maps: OS OL6, L96: GR 161978, GR 154975, GR 144952,
 GR 151956, GR 157954, GR 157953, GR 165971
Access point: Track to Devoke Water, GR 170796
Distance/ascent: 6¹/₂ mls/1900ft, 10km/580m
Approx time: 3¹/₂ hours

With Devoke Water and the distinct tops of White Pike and
Woodend Height already visible, a rusting signpost points to
the track from which a vaguely defined path breaks off right
up Rough Crag. The going levels before finally steepening to gain
the summit plateau. The summit cairn stands on pink-red granite.
Descend easily into the dip and rise again towards the summit of
Water Crag. The first rocky bump encountered has an in situ
cairn; the highest point lies just to the north. A path leads down to
cross Linbeck Gill falling from Devoke Water. Bear right to a large
circular pile of stones, a ruined shelter and a forlorn wooden post.
Bear first left then right to pick up the shoulder falling from White
Pike. Ascend this to a rocky lump. Move right to stand on a
pointed, twin-peaked rock outcrop with the next objective, The
Knott, now in view. Traverse the flanks of the hillside, over rock
and bracken and descend slightly. Cross a small gill, then ascend
to the shoulder plateau extending to The Knott. Cross the bog and
gain the tussocky grass rising to the rock outcrop summit. From
The Knott follow the grassy shoulder rising gently. Bear right at
the first outcrop to find a natural and well-defined corridor rising
easily through the steep ground. At its head bear right to the cairn,
precariously balanced on a knife edge. This marks the top of
White Pike. Rise towards Woodend Height, skirting the final
craggy outcrops to the left. Finally break through directly to the
summit point. Cross the summit and descend slightly to the rock
turret of Yoadcastle. Beneath an easy grassy descent crosses Hall
Beck and continues to the base of the fell. With the buildings of
Woodend Farm over to the right, an area of soft ground is crossed.

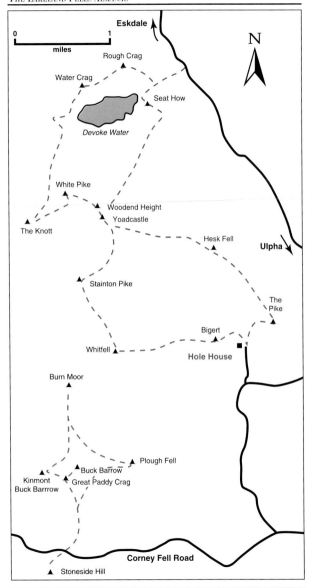

A gentle grassy flank, with numerous Cairns visible, leads to The Seat. Beyond this stands the rocky knoll of Seat How. Proceed, over a ruined stone wall, to ascend the easy eastern flank. Descend the same way. Take a clockwise circuit around the rocky outcrop before descending to the track.

THE PIKE, 1214FT/370M; HESK FELL, 1565FT/477M; YOADCASTLE, 1621FT/494M; STAINTON PIKE, 1632FT/498M; WHITFELL, 1881FT/573M; BIGERT, 1086FT/331M

Maps: OS OL6, L96: GR 186934, GR 176947, GR 157953, GR 153943, GR 159930, GR 176932
Access point: Hole House, restricted parking, GR 181930
Distance/ascent: 6¹/₂ mls/2065ft, 10km/630m
Approx time: 3¹/₂ hours

The surfaced road ends at a gate just over Holehouse Bridge. Follow the Side Pike farm track until a track leads off to the left. Follow it and take the gate to the right. Leave the track to follow the blunt nose rising up the open fellside above. Pass the stone remains of an old structure and continue across a ruined wall. Bear right beneath a small craggy outcrop. Another ruined wall rises steeply up the hillside. Follow this until a gap in the wall leads right. Climb to the top of The Pike. Follow the wall down the shoulder over the ruined wall. After the shoulder begins to ascend, a wooden gate will be found through the wall. Take it and continue along the other side of the wall until a further gate leads to the open fellside. Go straight up the flanks of Hesk Fell. The angle eases to reveal the extensive flat grass plain which is the summit of Hesk Fell. A few rocks form a poor cairn. Traverse the top and descend easily through tussocky grass and heather to the boggy col of Cockley Moss. Rise directly to a rocky outcrop with an in situ small stone wall, then bear right to the rocky peak of Yoadcastle.

Descend in the same direction, past the rock outcrop and ascend right, over a number of rocky knolls. Stride a wire fence in the dip beneath Stainton Pike. Ascend the rocky knoll of Stainton Pike. Strike a line south for Whitfell. Cross the wire fence just beyond Holehouse tarn. As the going begins to steepen, a slight path materialises. It leads directly to the substantial beehive cairn standing amidst a great circular mass of stones which mark the top of Whitfell. The trig point stands to the east, apparently at a slightly lower elevation. Proceed east on a quick descent down the nose of Whitfell to a gate in the wire fence by the ruined stone wall. An ancient track descending diagonally down the fellside merges from the left at this point. Follow it over Bigertmire Pasture before slightly boggy walking leads to a gate in a wire fence. The grass bump beyond this represents the top of Bigert. Take the gap in the ruined wall and descend the open fellside to the left to a track above the beck. Take the gate through the stone wall and follow it. Pass the hazels to an iron gate and the surfaced road just above Hole House.

GREAT PADDY CRAG, 1745FT/532M; BUCK BARROW, 1799FT/549M;
KINMONT BUCK BARROW, 1754FT/535M; BURN MOOR, 1780FT/543M;
PLOUGH FELL, 1470FT/448M; STONESIDE HILL, 1384FT/422M

Maps: OS P625, OL6, L96: GR 150909, GR 152910, GR 147910,
GR 151924, GR 162912, GR 146893
Access point: Corney Fell road summit, GR 150896
Distance/ascent: 5¹/₂ mls/110ft, 9km/335m
Approx time: 2¹/₂ hours

A wall rises to the north of the road. Take the track over open
fell on the right, passing the rock outcrops of Peg Crag and
Little Paddy Crag until the rocky bastion of Great Paddy Crag
looms above. To the right and beyond the rock pinnacles and
summit dome of Buck Barrow. Bear right around Great Paddy
Crag then cut back left, rising easily to the summit rock just above
the ruinous wall. A tiny cairn stands wedged in a triangular rocky
niche. Head directly for the summit cone of Buck Barrow, up easy
scree to reach the cairn standing on a point of rock.
    Descend the western flank of the cone and proceed to
circumnavigate around the bump of Great Paddy Crag. Cross a
ruined wall after which it is possible to strike rightwards to a gap
in another wall, blocked by a wooden palate. Cross the gap and
make gentle ascent to the summit cone of Kinmont Buck Barrow.
Descend to the north and move right to find a small wooden
gate/fence near the end of the stone wall. Climb this, (it won't
open), and cross a small stream to make boggy progress across the
col between Buck Barrow and Burn Moor. Easy ascent leads to the
slight rocky protruberance and cairn marking the top of the grassy
expanse of Burn Moor. Rapid descent leads to an easy traverse
along the 450m contour beneath Buckbarrow Crag to the summit
plateau of Plough Fell. A cairn stands on a rock just beyond its
eastern rim. Return to the slopes of Buck Barrow to find a high
rake leading diagonally up the fellside to Little Paddy Crag. From
Paddy Crag the track is followed back to the road. Beyond the road
a grassy shoulder leads to the steep-sided bump of Stoneside Hill.

35 BLACK COMBE GROUP

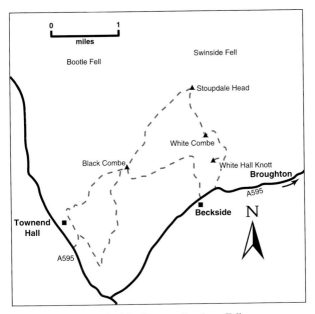

Location: Above the Duddon Estuary, Southern Fells.
Suggested Base: Whicham Valley.
Accommodation: *Whicham Valley:* limited facilities, self-catering and b&b; camping at Silecroft.

WHITE HALL KNOTT, 1020FT/311M; WHITE COMBE, 1361FT/415M;
STOUPDALE HEAD, 1548FT/472M; BLACK COMBE, 1970FT/600M; SOUTH
TOP of BLACK COMBE, 1926FT/587M

Maps: OS P625, L96: GR 156856, GR 155863, GR 151874,
    GR 135855, GR 136852
Access point: Beckside, car park by A595, GR 153847
Distance/ascent: 5¹/₂ mls/1970ft, 9km/600m
Approx time: 3¹/₂ hours

Follow the A595 for a short way up the hill then down towards the Fox and Goose Cottages, until a signpost reads 'Public Footpath White Combe'. A gate leads to a trackway and gates which lead to open, heavily-brackened fellside. After a short zigzag left the track, cut deep into the ground, rises to the right taking a diagonal line up the steep hillside. It divides in places to offer a

dual carriageway system. Near the shoulder of White Hall Knott
take the left, most direct, track to the col. Bear left and traverse
the grassy shoulder to make the final rise to the table top of White
Hall Knott. Return along the shoulder and ascend the trackway.
Bear left to the large circular mound of stones and the
cairn/shelter which marks the summit of White Combe. From here
take a direct, though pathless, line giving gentle grassy ascent to
Whitecombe Moss. Bear right to the highest point of the moss. A
tiny cairn of quartz rock marks the indistinct top of Stoupdale
Head. Follow a vague path over Whitecombe Head to traverse the
rim of Whitecombe Screes followed by Blackcombe Screes. Ascend
easily to the broad flat top of Black Combe. From its playing field
surface rises a triangulation point and a large circular shelter
cairn. Cross the dip holding the summit tarn and continue to the
large circular cairn which marks the South Top of Black Combe.
An easy grassy descent down the shoulder skirts the rim of the
combe. It steepens to gain the flat table area of Sty Knotts. A very
steep line is cut down beneath the central craggy outcrop and left
to the track along the narrow valley of Whitecombe Beck. Take the
stile above the charming cottages of the mill, through Ralliss Farm
back to Beckside.

BLACK COMBE, 1970FT/600M; SOUTH TOP of BLACK COMBE,
1926FT/587M

Maps: OS P625, L96: GR 135855, GR 136852
Access point: Lay-by on the south side of the A595, near
      Townend, GR 122837
Distance/ascent: 4¹/₂ mls/1855ft, 7.5km/565m
Approx time: 2¹/₂ hours

Opposite the lay-by a signpost 'Public Footpath Blackcombe'
points out the path through the thick bracken. It rises to the
left to skirt the hillside above a beech wood and traverses
above a wire fence. From the end of the fence it descends slightly
into Townend Gill. Cross the gill and descend slightly to a grass
track running along the stone wall. A little way before the
buildings of Whitbeck a distinct track rises through thick bracken
up the south shoulder of Millergill Beck. After a little ascent a
large boulder is passed. Beyond this the path begins to zigzag and
at the first turn a small detour left reveals the fine waterfall in
Millergill Beck. The path steepens until at a levelling in the
shoulder a vague path traverses left through thick heather. At the
first grass area in the heather, the path descends slightly before
continuing its horizontal traverse towards Miller Gill. It is now no
more than a narrow sheep trod. It gains the bed of the gill at its
widest point. Just above, a rocky outcrop on the north bank
shelters the ruins of an old shepherd's hut. The bed of the gill can
now be followed. Take the left fork until its furthest tentacle
touches the grassy track from Whicham. Cross the track and climb
to the summit shelter enclosing the concrete trig point. Proceed

TO BLACK COMBE FROM WHITE HALL KNOTT

south past the summit tarn to the cairn marking the South Top of
Black Combe. Descend directly to the west to pick up the grassy
track. Descend the main track to the edge of the Seaness table
top. This is found just beyond the point where the descent steepens
and a spring and stream appears to the left. Cross the table top to
the cairns marking the end of Seaness. Re-cross the plateau to a
distinct diagonal track. This leads down the hillside, above
Throstlerake Crag and beneath White Stones, towards the wood
beneath Townend.

36 OUTLYING EASTERN TOPS

Location: East of the main fells in the proximity Lakes Coniston
  and Windermere, Southern Fells.
Suggested Bases: Coniston and Bowness on Windermere.
Accommodation: Coniston: self-catering and b&b; limited
  facilities; Holly How and Coppermines House youth hostels;
  camping at Coniston Hall. *Bowness:* all facilities; Windermere
  youth hostel; camping at Tower Wood.

HOLME FELL, 1040FT/317M; BLACK CRAG on BLACK FELL, 1056FT/322M

Maps: OS OL7, L90, L96: GR 315006, GR 340016
Access point: Glen Mary Bridge, GR 321999
Distance/ascent: 6¾ mls/1690ft, 11km/515m
Approx time: 4 hours

Follow the road to the entrance of Yew Tree Farm. Proceed
down the drive over the bridge then take the track to the
right, bypassing the farmyard and skirting Penny House
Wood. Immediately beyond the wood pass through a gate and take
the path rising to the right. Enter Guards Wood above Yew Tree
Tarn. Continue along the path until the wood thins. Pass a
bouldery outcrop and follow a path that climbs steeply up to the
left to Uskdale Gap. This is the col on the long shoulder of Holme
Fell. A path rises to the left and leads up to the rock-slab rib of Ivy
Crag. A solid cairn marks the summit. Below to the west there's a
basin of heather. Beyond this lies the higher summit outcrop of
Holme Fell. Descend into the basin and cross it. Sink into a deep
corridor, which is a natural roadway with ancient tracks forking to
the left. One carries on through a miniature canyon. The other
rises to carry on south beneath the summit knoll. Follow the latter
for a short way then climb directly up the knoll by an obvious line
of weakness. The summit cairn is placed centrally on the raised
plateau.

Descend to the ancient trackway which falls from the corridor
and follow it around the side of a boggy hollow. Do not descend but
bear right. Pick a route through enclosing larch trees, and fall
slightly to a stone walled dam. Cross the dam along the top of one
of the outside stone walls, avoiding the void in the centre. At the
far side the path skirts around to a higher pond. Follow its shore,
past the small retaining dam, then break left down the hill past an
old quarry to the right. Follow the old track down to a larger track
and bear right. After a gate the large hole of Hodge Close Quarry
appears. The path bears right to the right of a wire protective
fence. The path joins a track just above a pond to the left. Turn
right and follow the track through High Oxenfell Farm after which
it becomes a surfaced road. Bear left past Low Oxenfell and
continue to a junction and the main A593 Ambleside to Coniston
road. On the far side of the road a track rises through a small

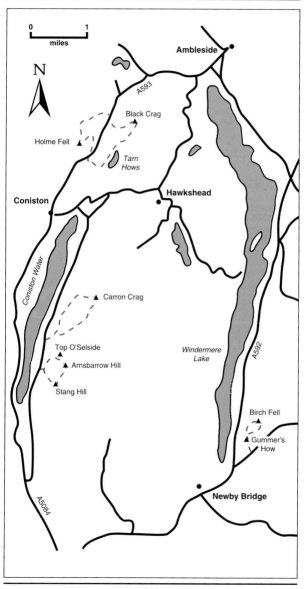

larch wood. It then opens out onto fields on the fellside known as Hollin Bank. The track skirts the wall falling slightly to cross a stream before rising again. Climb to the top of the field and take a gate through the stone wall to the left. Pass a large boulder and bear right, to join another track. Pass through a further gate with the building of Low Arnside below to the right. The track continues through another gate. It descends slightly then rises alongside a stone wall to the fell gate. After a small knoll with larch trees growing on it, a grassy track bears off left. Cross a low boggy area, with Iron Keld Crag to the right and ascend slightly. The track levels and a steep path rises up the grassy bank to the right to a small cairn. A vague path leads to the final pull, by a stone wall, up the western flank of Black Crag. Descend south to the shoulder and follow the path down to the edge of a dark conifer plantation. A gate/stile gives access to a rough track descending through Iron Keld Plantation to emerge into an open track. Turn right with fine larch trees standing to the right. Do not take any gates to the left until after descending a steep hill. A well-signed gate/stile on the left provides a path to Tarn Hows. At the base of the tarn follow a path down the true right bank of the stream which issues from it. Descent leads to a footbridge and the car park.

CARRON CRAG, 1030FT/314M

Maps: OS OL6, L96: GR 325943
Access point: Park-A-Moor National Trust car park, GR 299927
Distance/ascent: 5¹/₂ mls/1215ft, 9km/370m
Approx time: 3¹/₄ hours

A track leaves the back of the parking area to pass a stone barn. Above the gate, a few steps and a stile lead into the oak woods. Follow the track rising up through the wood until at a ruined stone wall the track forks. Take the right branch, which is overgrown and boggy at first, to cross a small stream. Traversing beneath a field the track rises to a gate. Take the stile left of the gate and continue up the field until near the top a stile climbs the wire fence by two old slate gateposts, one standing, one fallen. This joins an old lane. Although the lane can be followed from the bottom of the field it is best avoided as described because it is extremely boggy. Follow the lane, with a stream on the left, to the unsurfaced track which contours the hillside.

This rough track rises from distant High Nibthwaite, providing the only access to Low Parkamoor Farm. Turn left through the gate and follow the track to the deserted farm and on to a stile and gate. Turn left and follow the undulating grassy track that weaves its way through boggy hollows and rocky knolls up onto the high shoulder of The Park. The track leads into the forest via a stile and gate. The track enters a corridor between high forest fencing and begins to descend. Dead ahead, the top of Carron Crag can be seen (at the time of writing sufficent trees had

been felled to allow this). Intercept a main forest road and bear
left. In a few hundred yards to the right there is a forestry break.
Those wishing to keep their journey to a minimum should cross the
ditch and follow it. Those preferring a longer but easier walk may
follow the main track for perhaps a kilometre. At a junction it is
possible to bear right to gain the track passing the northern end of
Carron Crag.

NB: the author accepts no reponsibility for those getting lost
on this latter option! It should also be noted that on the OS map,
tracks and completely overgrown firebreaks are indistinguishable.
Following the firebreak is not easy, although at the time of writing
the trees to the right had all been felled.

Emerge onto a track and bear left; take a right fork and
emerge onto an even better track. Turn right and in a little way
find a gate and path leading up the north end of Carron Crag. An
observation post straddles the rock. A trig point stands at the
northern point. Follow the path down the southern end of the fell
to emerge through a gate onto a level track. At the junction bear
right and descend slightly into a dip. As the track rises again you
reach a further junction. Tracks go left and right but our way lies
across the junction. An ancient path rises over the flanks of
Mustard Hill. Levelling, the path again meets a forestry track.
Cross this to follow another forest track bearing down the hill in a
southerly direction. At the bottom there's a triangular junction.
Proceed past the junction and carry on in the same direction for a
short way, until a path veers off to the right. Follow this over
Farra Grain Gill and through dense conifer to emerge into the
blinding light of the open moor at a gate. The boggy track crosses
the moor to meet a stone wall. Follow the line of the wall to
intercept the track serving Low Parkamoor.

STANG HILL, 1037FT/316M; ARNSBARROW HILL, 1056FT/322M; TOP
O'SELSIDE, 1099FT/335M

Maps: OS OL6, L96: GR 310908, GR 311911, GR 309919
Access point: Nibthwaite National Trust car park, GR 296908
Distance/ascent: 3mls/1100ft, 5km/335m
Approx time: 2 hours

At the top left corner of the car park an ancient track rises
through the woods. In a short way an ancient walled lane
branches off to the left. Ignore this and rise with the track
until it crests a hill and falls slightly to the right. When the track
forks, rise to the left. Exit the wood over a stile into the rough road
from the hamlet of High Nibthwaite. Turn right up the road until it
makes a sharp bend. Continue straight on following a small path to
the left of the stream. Cross the stream and rise up the brackened
hillside to pass the end of a stone walled field to the right. Shortly
join a well-defined path which traverses the hillside. Bear right
along this path which has arisen from High Bethecar. At the closest
point to the summit an ascent can be made of Stang Hill. The top is

OVER CONISTON WATER LOOKING FROM THE PARK

marked by a cairn. Cross the heathery divide to the craggy top of Arnsbarrow Hill.

Descend the shoulder. Circumnavigate little Neile Stove Crag, to pass over boggy ground beneath the foot of Arnsbarrow Tarn. Rise up the grassy flanks of Top O'Selside to enter a little corridor then bear right to climb the heather-strewn rocky knoll and its grassy domed summit topped by a cairn. Descend to the west from the summit into a little heathery bowl and exit to the left. An easy and direct descent down the shoulder reaches the point where the footpath from High Bethecar and the rough road from High Nibthwaite intercept. Bear left along the road to take the stile entering the wood.

GUMMER'S HOW, 1054FT/321M; BIRCH FELL, 1043FT/318M

Maps: OS P626, L96: GR 390885, GR 395892
Access point: Astley's Plantation car park, GR 390877
Distance/ascent: 2^1/$_2$ mls/590ft, 4km/180m
Approx time: 1^1/$_2$ hours

From the car park ascend the road to the kissing gate on the left. The path is broad and unmistakable. Pass silver birch and ancient larch to rise over polished rock slabs to the stone trig point which marks the summit. From the trig point a path heads north and descends alongside a few larch trees. Bear right and descend east to the edge of a boggy hollow. A small slate quarry lies just to the left near the bottom. Turn left along the edge of the bog. A path, which has been unused for some time, lies just above. Walk to a ruined wall, the old path takes a constructed gateway through this, but turn right to ascend by the wall which rises up the flanks of Birch Fell. After crossing a ruined wall weave through a jumble of larch. Bear left to join a wire fence. This rises over the rocky summit knoll of Birch Fell. Pick a line through the larch down the southern flank of the fell until it is possible to bear right to the edge of the boggy hollow. A high line can be picked over a series of rocky outcrops which allow a relatively dry crossing. Beyond the hollow, by the corner of the plantation, intercept a good grass path. It follows the edge of the pines descending to the original broad path.

INDEX OF TOPS

Page number refers to first mention of the top in the book.